The Wandering Fool
&
Three Lectures on Hermeticism

THE
WANDERING FOOL

or

LOVE AND ITS SYMBOLS:
EARLY STUDIES ON THE TAROT

By the Anonymous Author
of
Meditations on the Tarot

&

THREE LECTURES ON
HERMETICISM

By
Robert Powell

⊕

Logo Sophia
San Rafael Ca

First published in the USA
by LogoSophia
an imprint of Sophia Perennis
Lectures © Robert Powell 2009
Text translation © James Wetmore 2009

Series editor: James R. Wetmore

For information, address:
LogoSophia, P.O. Box 151011
San Rafael, CA 94915

Library of Congress Cataloging-in-Publication Data

Mat itinerant. English.
The wandering fool: love and its symbols: early studies on
the tarot / by the anonymous author of Meditations
on the tarot & three lectures on hermeticism;
[lectures] by Robert Powell.

p. cm.
Includes bibliographic references.
ISBN 978 1 59731 500 5 (pbk: alk. paper)
1. Tarot. 2. Hermetism. I. Powell, Robert, 1947– II. Title
BF1879.T2M36713 2009
133.3'2424—dc22   2009023142

CONTENTS

Author's Foreword to *Meditations on the Tarot* i

Introduction

    By Robert Powell iii
    Adapted from Kairos edition iv
    Adapted from Achamoth edition vi
    Acknowledgments viii

Part One: Three Lectures on Hermeticism

    Lecture I (2006) 1
    Lecture II (2007) 22
    Lecture III (2008) 40

Part Two: The Wandering Fool

    Arcanum XIV: Temperance 71
    Arcanum XV: The Devil 77
    Arcanum XVI: The Tower 82
    Arcanum XVII: The Star 87
    Arcanum XVIII: The Moon 91
    Arcanum XIX: The Sun 96
    Arcanum XX: Judgment (Resurrection) 100
    Arcanum XXI/Zero: The Fool (The Jester) 106
    Arcanum XXII (XXI): The World 111

The Cards of the Major Arcana 117

Author's Foreword to
Meditations on the Tarot

These meditations on the Major Arcana of the Tarot are Letters addressed to the Unknown Friend. The addressee in this instance is anyone who will read all of them and who thereby acquires definite knowledge, through the experience of meditative reading, about Christian Hermeticism. He will know also that the author of these Letters has said more about himself in these Letters than he would have been able to in any other way. No matter what other source he might have, he will know the author better through the Letters themselves.

These Letters are written in French because in France—since the eighteenth century until the present time, i.e. the second half of the twentieth century there exists a literature on the Tarot, a phenomenon which is found nowhere else. On the other hand, there existed in France—and it still persists—a continuous *tradition* of Hermeticism, in which is united a spirit of free research with one of respect for the tradition. The purpose of these Letters therefore will be to "incarnate" into this tradition, i.e. to become an organic part of it, and in this way to contribute support to it.

As these Letters are intended only to serve, to sustain, and to support the Hermetic tradition from its first appearance in the epoch of Hermes Trismegistus, lost in the remoteness of antiquity and become legendary—they are a definite manifestation of this millennial-old current of thought, effort, and revelation. Their aim is not only to revive the tradition in the twentieth century but also, and above all, to immerse the reader (or rather the Unknown Friend) in this current—be it temporarily or for ever. For this reason the numerous citations of ancient and modern authors which you will find in these Letters are not due to literary considerations, nor to a display of erudition. They are *evocations* of the masters of the tradition, in order that they may be present with their impulses of aspiration and their light of thought in the current of meditative thought which these Letters on the twenty-two Major Arcana of the Tarot represent. For these are in essence twenty-two spiritual exercises, by means of which you, dear Unknown Friend, will immerse yourself in the current of the living tradition, and thus enter into the community of spirits who have served it and who are still serving it.

And the citations in question only serve the aim of a "relief setting" for this community. For the links in the chain of the tradition are not thoughts and efforts alone; they are above all *living beings* who were thinking these thoughts and willing these efforts. The essence of the tradition is not a doctrine, but rather a community of spirits from age to age.

There remains nothing more to say in this introduction to the Letter-Meditations on the Tarot, because all other questions concerning them will find a response in the letters themselves.

Your friend greets you,
dear Unknown Friend,
from beyond the grave

Introduction

The foregoing words by the anonymous author of *Meditations on the Tarot* serve also as an Introduction to this publication, which comprises two parts. Part I comprises three lectures held by Robert Powell, the translator of *Meditations on the Tarot* into English from the original French manuscript. These lectures, held in California in 2006, 2007, and 2008, were delivered to an audience of friends of Christian Hermeticism, who gather every year to converse and share concerning the path of Christian Hermeticism. The second lecture, in particular, serves as an introduction to Part II of this publication, which is a translation into English, from the original French, of notes made by the author of *Meditations on the Tarot* as preliminary studies of the Tarot prior to his writing the book itself, published here under the title *The Wandering Fool*. By way of explanation concerning these preliminary studies, herewith a paragraph from the second lecture:

> The method followed by the author of *Meditations on the Tarot* was something he developed in his preliminary studies of the images of the Tarot cards. This methodology has now been revealed through the inclusion of material published in this volume for the first time in English translation. This material comprises notes made by the author of *Meditations on the Tarot*. These were his preparatory notes before writing the book—and these reveal his method. Unfortunately, the notes cover only the last nine Arcana, from XIV to XXII. The notes to the first thirteen Arcana have gone missing.

Also included are two further Introductions: one based on the Introduction to the Luxembourg (Kairos) edition of *The Wandering Fool* and one adapted from the Introduction to the German (Achamoth) edition, which was published under the title *Inspirations to the Major Arcana of the Tarot XIV-XXII*.

ROBERT POWELL

From the Introduction to the Kairos Edition

*(Le Mat Itinerant: L'Amour et ses symboles
Une Méditation chrétienne sur le Tarot, Luxembourg, 2007)*

The handwritten originals of the sketches presented in this volume are preserved in the archives of the 'Ramstein Circle' in Trier, Germany. The author, whose mother tongue was Russian, wrote these notes in French. Since they were not intended for publication in their present form, the author never went over them with an eye to style or syntax. Minor editorial modifications in layout, syntax, and punctuation have been made occasionally, but only where it seemed useful for the sake of clarity and unity of presentation. Such changes were made only where there could be absolutely no doubt as to the author's intent. As a matter of principle, any portions of the text where there might be room for interpretation as to meaning have been left unchanged. A critical edition of this text, illustrating the author's later development of some its themes, would no doubt be quite a revealing enterprise and open up new dimensions of understanding. However, that is not the object of the present edition, which is rather to let the text to speak for itself.

The author of this text remains little-known. As he requested, his best-known work, *Meditations on the Tarot*, was published anonymously, as from one 'beyond the grave.' But precisely on this account we remain understandably keen to know more about him and the life-journey that led him, both outwardly and inwardly, through Slavic, Anglo-Germanic, and Latin Europe. He lived in Russia, Estonia, Holland, Germany, England, and finally on the Spanish island of Mallorca, where he died. This extraordinary European's spiritual horizon was broad indeed: youthful studies of French and Russian Hermeticists led him in due course to Rudolf Steiner's Anthroposophy, and then, following World War II, to Catholicism. To this we may add also his deep engagement (although he was raised a Lutheran) with Orthodox Christianity, as well as with the great religions and spiritual traditions of the East.

Introduction

Throughout his life, our author continued to employ and integrate what he had learned at each spiritual station along his path, so that, even after becoming a Catholic, he made rich use of hermetic symbols and anthroposophical thought-forms. Thus, what might on superficial acquaintance seem to be shifts or breaks in his path can be viewed as elements of a larger, organic whole.

The stages along this path are sufficiently attested to by his published and also his unpublished writings, as well as manuscripts of his lectures. He did not write as an academic theologian or philosopher. Rather, his sole purpose was to offer a meditative path founded upon contemplative vision and symbols. Hans Urs von Balthasar, a pre-eminent Catholic theologian of the twentieth century, considered the author 'a Christian thinker of the most compelling purity.' Indeed, in his works—which he himself described as spiritual exercises—thought and prayer are united: they are more an invitation to contemplation than an effort to convince the reasoning mind.

The present text, published in this volume under the title *The Wandering Fool*, dates from the 1950s. Of the original 22 sketches (one for each of the Major Arcana of the Tarot) only those published here are extant. Although the author did not intend them for publication, it has nevertheless seemed proper to make them available at this time, in view both of the wide impact of his masterwork *Meditations on the Tarot*, and of their wonderfully pregnant and poetic character.

In all his works, our author returns repeatedly to the question how human beings of our time can find within themselves the source of revelation, the place where contraries resolve into unity—the inner space where reason and belief, intelligence and reason, external authority and authentic inner experience, no longer oppose each other, but join together. Caught as we so often are today between the relativism of subjectivity and the dogmatism of objectivity, many despair of ever finding the source of meaning and truth. No wonder, then, that the author of *Meditations on the Tarot* chose to reach out directly at particular places in the *Meditations*, addressing the reader as 'dear unknown friend'.

For he is addressing himself to those who, like him, never cease to question and seek: that is, to free spirits on the quest for their 'star', for the sources of faith; to those who yearn for and sorely miss access to the living fount of inner conviction and truth; to those 'crying in the wilderness'—to those who, like the Hanged Man of the XIIth Arcanum, wait in hope that their parched and often fruitless efforts might finally bear gifts of joy.

From the Introduction to the Achamoth Edition

(Inspirationen ʒu den Grossen Arcana des Taro XIV–XXII, Germany, 2007)

The Tarot depicts human qualities and virtues that must be transformed in order that they may assimilate the Christ and become a vessel for His activity. Although the Tarot predates Christianity, the Hermetic path from which it comes can be considered as a Christian path dating from before the time of Christ's incarnation, in the sense that its teaching was intended to enable human souls to take into themselves the great Sun Being, Christ, even prior to His incarnation.

The reason there are 22 Arcana of the Tarot is that human beings are endowed with 7 virtues, 12 capacities, and 3 qualities, all of which must be created anew by each individual. These virtues, capacities, and qualities are explicitly described in the author's *Meditations on the Tarot*.

If we seek the source of inspiration underlying *Meditations on the Tarot*, we come to a great individuality who in one of his incarnations, under the name Christian Rosenkreutz, lived during the fifteenth century, when the Tarot originated (see page 23). From life to life this individuality never ceases his labor directed toward bringing humanity into relationship with Christ. For Christian Rosenkreutz has always—from incarnation to incarnation—lived as an exemplary model of this path, regardless whether humanity takes any notice of it or not—and this in spite of all that Rudolf Steiner, through his anthroposophical teachings, has tried to communicate to humanity on this important subject. The mission of Christian Rosenkreutz is to lead all human souls to such a depth of inwardness that their hearts may blossom into an 'inner Sun'—as is so profoundly described in the last Arcanum of *Meditations on the Tarot*, 'The World'.

Those familiar with the Tarot may find it hard to accept that it is linked here with an institution, the Church. But in truth its ultimate origin is the spiritual world: the spiritual hierarchies, as well as the guiding Holy Trinity. From this wellspring comes the ancient wisdom-teaching underlying Hermeticism: 'As above, so below.'

At the source of the Tarot stands a great wise one, who both conceived this teaching and throughout the ages mediates it to humanity. This teacher of the Tarot generally remains hidden from us. Clearly, the one who originally brought the wisdom of the Tarot and its imagery possessed knowledge of the origins of the world and of humanity. In Hermes Trismegistus, the teacher of the Egyptians, this wise one stands before us. The great Hermes Trismegistus, originator of the wisdom of Hermeticism, took up the work of teaching again in the twentieth century—this time completed through the Divine Son, Jesus Christ. In the present age, now at a time of humanity's most acute need, he bears aloft the light of eternity. And although he must also bear across the abyss that separates the eternal from the temporal the burden of those who doubt and scoff, he still conveys to the world his power of love, which calls to new life the ancient wisdom-teaching: 'That which is below will become like unto that which is above.' And so this work stands again in the arena of God's creation.

The concentrated sketches offered in this text may be considered as preliminary studies for the author's later masterwork *Meditations on the Tarot*. Despite their brevity, the themes developed here constitute a unified whole. This is why it was considered justified to publish them, although this was not the author's original intent when he wrote them.

To better understand the author's motivation in composing his work on the Tarot, we include here his introduction to *Meditations on the Tarot* (see pages i–ii) as well as the following excerpt from a letter (dated May 31, 1967) to some close friends of his:

> My meditations on the Tarot are no scientific undertaking. Rather, they are a repeated and wide-ranging effort, by means of the symbolism of the Hermetic tradition, to enter again deeply into the all-encompassing stream of the Catholic tradition, in such a way that, through a shift in perspective, through a purifying atonement, the Catholic and the Hermetic traditions might be seen as one, in harmony with each other.

Acknowledgments

The publisher would like to thank Robert Powell not only for the three lectures contained in this volume, but also for his assistance refining the translation of the text of the *Wandering Fool* and for other editorial assistance. Special thanks are due also to John Hipsley for his transcriptions and revisions of the lectures, and to Philip Mees for helping make this edition possible. Grateful acknowledgment is also given to the authors of the introductory material of the Kairos edition (*Le Mat itinerant*), Friederike Migneco and Volker Zotz, and to Willi Seiß, author of the introductory material for the Achamoth edition (*Inspirationen zu den Großen Arcana des Taro XIV–XXII*).

JAMES WETMORE

PART ONE

Three Lectures

on

Hermeticism

by

Robert Powell

given in

2006, 2007, and 2008

I

Hermeticism Lecture
2006

I would like to welcome everyone to this meeting today, where we all have in common the extraordinary book, *Meditations on the Tarot*.

We are addressed by the author as "Dear unknown friends." It is wonderful to come together with friends—known and unknown—at this special moment in time in the unfolding of the impulse underlying this work. Next year (2007) will commemorate the fortieth year since the completion of this work by the anonymous author. And we are also very close to completion of 33⅓ years since the author's death. Those of you who know my book *Chronicle of the Living Christ* will understand the significance of this special rhythm—the exact length of Jesus Christ's life from birth to resurrection. This is an important biographical rhythm, that of birth and resurrection in life's unfolding.

Part of the motivation for coming together at this time is to focus on a new level, for a resurrection impulse is approaching in relation to the work with *Meditations on the Tarot*. This is indeed a joyous occasion.

Translation History

In this introduction I would like to focus on what for me has been the essence of working with *Meditations on the Tarot*. First, though, a few words about how it came about that I translated this work. In 1978, in Amsterdam, I met an elderly woman. During our meeting, she brought out the manuscript, which was in French, and said "You are the one to translate this into English." The ensuing work of translation continued over the next four years, during which time I was inwardly guided and became aware that this work was written by a spiritual master—someone with whom one could converse and put questions.

Since that time I have met many people who have had the same or a similar experience. In taking the book into our hands, we can have an immediate connection with the author in spiritual realms. *Meditations on the Tarot* is what the author left behind in this world as a means for coming into connection with him in spiritual realms.

This raises the question: Who is the author? I do not mean: What was his name? Rather, I mean who was he in a deeper sense, in the context of humankind's spiritual evolution? I would like to offer some thoughts on this. As it is an anonymous work, evidently there was no value placed by the author on putting forward his personality. With him it is clearly a matter of working to awaken the higher soul and spiritual nature in human beings.

That is his work. As someone who might be called a "friend of Christ," he works as one able to lead us into connection with Christ. This is the signature of *Meditations on the Tarot*: to awaken us to our higher spiritual calling.

Encounter with a Stranger

Interesting accounts have been given by various people of their meetings—on a spiritual level—with the author of this work. One such account can be found in the preface to *Healing into Immortality*, by the New York psychiatrist Gerald Epstein, who describes there an experience in 1974 while he was with his teacher in Jerusalem drinking tea in her garden. A thin bespectacled gentleman walking by stopped for a moment and said in a booming voice: "It reminds me of the days of the prophecies." His next encounter with this stranger was in January 1986 in a New York esoteric bookstore, The Paraclete Bookshop. He was interested in mental imagery and had selected several volumes from the bookstore shelves. He was about to pay for them when this same stranger, without saying a word, picked up each book in turn and laid it down again, as if to say "This is not it; this is not it." He did this with every book. Then the stranger pointed to a copy of *Meditations on the Tarot*. Dr. Epstein decided to buy this book and forego the others. He went to the door of the bookshop to thank the stranger, who had just left. When he got outside the stranger was gone.

Dr. Epstein writes in his preface of his conviction that it was an Angel that had guided him to the book. When he began reading it, his life was changed. A stream of inspiration began to flow and his questions began to be answered inwardly.

This example is an illustration concerning the book *Meditations on the Tarot*, whose author attached no importance to details of his own personality. Working beyond the level of personality, he can be thought of as a friend and guide of humanity, one who is able to help each one of us spiritually if we are seeking a path of spiritual development.

The Path of the Heart

The beginning of this path is described in the first Arcanum (chapter 1) of *Meditations on the Tarot*. The essence of this beginning is "concentration without effort," where the heart becomes the center of consciousness; this is the central purpose of the first Arcanum.

The path begins with the heart. In a discreet way, using words that can easily be overlooked, the author indicates the stream to which he belongs. In the first Arcanum he writes of John—the beloved disciple who listened to the beating of the Master's heart—that he was, is, and always will be the representative and guardian of the heart.

As such he was not, is not, and never will be the *leader* or *head* of the Church. Just as the heart is not called upon to replace the head, so is John not called upon to succeed Peter. The mission of John is to keep the light and soul of the Church alive until the Second Coming of the Lord. This is why John has never claimed, and never will claim, the office of directing the body of the Church. He vivifies this body, but he does not direct its actions.

In working with *Meditations on the Tarot*, we are connecting to the stream of John. The following is from the invitation everyone received for today's meeting.

> One is free if one works with *symbols* rather than predetermined concepts—with symbols that are multifaceted—or, at least, if one considers the concepts themselves as symbols and works with them correspondingly. Symbols—from sources such as the *Tabula Smaragdina*, Revelation, the Kabbalah, the Arcana of the Tarot—offer a stimulus. At the same time, this is a stimulus leading in a certain direction (as with well-formulated questions in human conversation), namely a stimulus to recognize and know the supersensible in a way—and in the right measure—suitable for each individual's needs and capabilities. Concepts—many concepts—which are clear and sharp, can be developed from symbols. However, symbols never run dry through conceptualization, because they are *ways* to reality and not the results of a drawing back from reality, as is the case with abstraction. Symbols do not enslave. They "ask" and "say" exactly as much as the person in question wants and is capable of receiving. They leave the human being completely free. And this is also the most important reason why those who speak of the supersensible from experience do so in symbols. They want to communicate with people in such a way that human beings not only remain free, but become even *freer* (and more *creative*). John, who wrote Revelation, spoke in this way. Revelation has existed for almost two thousand years and continues to live on. Has it ever enslaved anyone? An inquisition has never arisen on account of symbolism, or through symbolism, whereas every conceptual system of necessity strives to exercise a reign of total dominance over human beings. . . . It is a matter of a quiet *mystery stream* without any pretensions, which wants neither to dominate nor to instruct, but exercises inwardly—in a way that draws upon the stream of the mysteries—an enlivening, spiritualizing, healing influence in an

indirect way. Just as symbols do not instruct, but rather stimulate, so should a modern mystery stream work like a symbol in the world—not instructing, but *stimulating*.

I have translated this from a letter that was written in German by the author of *Meditations on the Tarot* on July 30, 1956, where references are made to the spiritual exercises of the 22 Arcana; and it gives the example of Revelation, which consists of 22 chapters with corresponding images. This work of John is something that has never become cause for dogma or strife, because it is presented in such a way—in the form of images—that we are left completely free. We can look upon the 22 images of the 22 Major Arcana of *Meditations on the Tarot* in much the same way as we can the images presented by John in the 22 chapters of Revelation.

In fact, these Tarot images are in our time a metamorphosis of what was given nineteen centuries ago as the images comprising the 22 chapters of Revelation. There is an inner correspondence between the 22 Arcana of *Meditations on the Tarot* and the chapters of Revelation, so that if you are working with the first Arcanum, there is a correspondence with the central image from the first chapter of Revelation. The Magician of the first Arcanum is a powerful image that takes us to another level, another plane of existence—as does the central image of chapter 1 of Revelation.

Arcana are Icons

As indicated by the author in the ninth chapter of *Meditations on the Tarot*, the Arcana of the Tarot are inscribed in spiritual realms. They are archetypes, and we can find a living relationship with them. It is the same with the images in Revelation. The Arcana are icons—windows to a higher spiritual reality—through which we come into a higher level of cognition of spiritual realities. We can open ourselves to them. As with all true icons, they are not just windows; they are also aspects of ourselves. This is one way we can work with an Arcanum: we can step into it, identifying ourselves with it.

With this work we are called to a path of spiritual transformation, a path of initiation. This is set forth in the very first Arcanum, which is the *Arcanum of the Arcana*—the key to all the other Arcana. First we prepare ourselves inwardly in silence, and then we focus upon the image of the Arcanum with devotion—opening ourselves to it as if we were contemplating an icon (for example, an icon of Christ or the Virgin Mary).

Devotion is a key that unlocks the mystery concealed in the Arcanum. If we allow our heartfelt longing for connection with spiritual reality to well up within us, something begins to open through our devotion as a magical key.

The first Arcanum clearly brings to expression that this work is a path of service. It is not for financial gain or power over other people. The impulse of Christian Hermeticism is to serve God: to find our true calling and mission as human beings.

Central Focus is the Meeting with Christ

How can we work with this book? It opens up a path of service through our devotion. On this path it is very important that we have a central focus. This is attained through concentration—"concentration without effort"—which leads to the great initiation, a meeting with Christ.

The archetype of this spiritual encounter is depicted in the first chapter of Revelation, where an extraordinary encounter of John with the Risen Christ is described. As a focus for our meeting, let us contemplate the relevant words from the first chapter of Revelation, evoking the central focus at the core of *Meditations on the Tarot*.

John is a forerunner of humanity. What John lived through nineteen hundred years ago on the island of Patmos was a prefiguration of what is now possible for all humanity, if we truly seek the great initiation—the meeting with Christ.

When studying *Meditations on the Tarot*, it is a powerful help always to hold this central focus in consciousness. This is the goal. Through this work the meeting or encounter with Christ—the great initiation—is possible. And the archetype of this meeting we find described in the first chapter of Revelation. This, essentially, is the content of the first Arcanum.

The First of the Seven Seals of Revelation

The first Arcanum is also the first Seal. In this encounter, Christ is experienced no longer as a human being, for, having passed through the Ascension, He is a cosmic being:

Whose hair is white as snow-white wool—a sign of cosmic wisdom.

From whose mouth proceeds a sharp two-edged sword—the sword of the word; for the good and against evil.

Whose face shines like the sun—these are the sun-like qualities of the heart that have risen into the head.

Whose eyes are like flames of fire—burning with the fire of divine love and thus able to see through the veil of appearances and cognize spirit in all matter.

Whose voice is like the sound of rushing water—this is the power of the Word that brought all things into existence.

Around whose breast is a golden girdle—the outer sign of what is addressed in the first Arcanum as the opening of the heart; this is the power of love burning to unite with the Divine: true mysticism.

Who is clothed in a long white robe—his body is purified and radiates out with the light of purity ("white").

Whose right hand holds seven stars—he has become master of the planetary forces that are also mentioned in the seventh Arcanum.

Whose feet are like burnished bronze refined as in a furnace—he walks on the earth with the power of divine will radiating through his feet, linking heaven and earth.

This is the goal expressed both in the image of the first Seal and in the first Arcanum. It is an image of what we are to become through bringing to realization the words "Not I, but Christ in me" (Galatians 2:20). This is the goal and essence toward which we can strive in the future. We are invited to go through a transformation to become "sons and daughters of light" or "children of God," as expressed in the Gospels (Romans 8:20).

This is the central focus of the work on the path of Christian Hermeticism, as outlined by the author of *Meditations on the Tarot*. The author is one who is able to lead us on this path, for he has himself traveled this path as a "friend of Christ." He has a consciousness that extends to all human beings on this planet.

In writing this work, the author was conscious of those who would need to find it, knowing that they would recognize the voice that speaks through it, and that this voice is bringing a message of love and an opening of the heart. It is also about the path of uniting the ancient Egyptian mysteries with Christianity.

Let us now return again to the question of the identity of the author of this work. In a discreet way it is described in the 21st Arcanum—the Fool. However, one has to read between the lines.

Intellectuality Fused with Spirituality

For those of you who know the work well, the twenty-first Arcanum is about the uniting of the head and the heart. This is the goal of the attainment of concentration without effort, where our guiding consciousness moves from the head to the heart, signifying the fusion of intellectuality with spirituality.

The leader or teacher who guides us on this path is the one who is known in the Buddhist tradition as the successor of Gautama (the founder of Buddhism)—the Maitreya (literally "the bearer of the Good"). The Maitreya is the Bodhisattva who is to appear as a Buddha 5,000 years after the death of Gautama. If you read what the author describes in Chapter Twenty-One of *Meditations on the Tarot*, you will see that this whole work is in the stream of the Maitreya Buddha. What is revealed in this chapter—something never revealed before—is that the Maitreya Buddha is one and the same as the Kalki Avatar: the one who is awaited in the Hindu tradition as the next Avatar. Krishna was the eighth Avatar. Kalki is considered to be the tenth and last Avatar or incarnation of Vishnu.

I would like to read the following prediction concerning the coming of the Kalki Avatar.

> By the time the age of Kali ends . . . religious principles will be ruined. . . . So-called religion will be mostly atheistic. . . . The occupations of men will be stealing, lying, and needless violence, and all the social classes will be reduced to the lowest level. . . . Family ties will extend no further than the immediate bonds of marriage . . . homes will be devoid of piety, and all human beings will have become like asses.

> At that time the supreme personality of the Godhead will appear on the earth. Acting with the power of pure spiritual goodness, he will rescue eternal religion. Lord Kalki will appear in . . . the great soul of Vishnu Yasha. . . . When the Supreme Lord has appeared on earth as Kalki, the maintainer of religion, then Satya Yuga will begin, and human society will bring forth progeny in the mode of goodness. (*Srimad Bhagavatam* 12.2.16–23)

Vishnu Yasha ("possessing God's glory") is the name given in this text to the human being who will be the bearer of the Kalki Avatar.

This is the prophecy of the end of the age of Kali Yuga. Kali Yuga (Devanagari, literally "Age of Kali", "age of vice") is one of the four stages of development that the world goes through as part of the cycle of yugas described in Hindu scriptures—the others being the Satya Yuga, Treta Yuga, and Dvapara Yuga. What is the Kali Yuga? One way to look at it is that we have reached its end.[1]

It is clear to everyone who reads *Meditations on the Tarot* that its author is concerned with the renewal of true religion—the reuniting of humanity with the Divine. When he refers to the  Church, he has on the one hand the external manifestation in view, but is also holding in view the Eternal Church. This latter is a great hierarchy of beings extending from the Father, Son, and Holy Spirit, through all the celestial hierarchies —Seraphim, Cherubim, Thrones, Dominions, Virtues, Powers, Principalities, Archangels, and Angels. This is the Eternal Church.

The outer Church should be a reflection of the Eternal Church. If we look at the original founding impulse proceeding from Christ and working through the apostles, it is evident that originally there was a true reflection of the Eternal Church. This is why the author—in the spirit of Kalki, the "maintainer of religion"— connects onto the stream of the Church, to help bring the original founding impulse alive again in our time.

In using the term Kalki Avatar, we must distinguish between "the supreme personality of the Godhead" and the human being who is its bearer and whose task for the future is the restoration of true religion. His mission is to bring forth progeny of the future in the mode of goodness. Here we see the link with the Maitreya as "the bearer of the Good." The essence of our work with *Meditations on the Tarot* is that it enable us to connect to this great stream in the service of the Good.

1. For a discussion concerning the end of Kali Yuga in 1899 (or, alternatively, in 2012), see Robert Powell and Kevin Dann, *Christ and the Maya Calendar* (Gt. Barrington, MA: SteinerBooks, 2009).

Study of Meditations on the Tarot: *The First Arcanum*

Step 1—Mysticism

In studying *Meditations on the Tarot*, we need to look at the whole sequence of the Arcana—or at least at all 22 Major Arcana of the Tarot. It is the first Arcanum above all that deals with the great initiation and our becoming conscious on a higher spiritual level. On the journey through each Arcanum we travel the path from one Arcanum to the next. The ideal is that, while studying individually, we are also able to meet as a community in the spirit. At our meeting today we can endeavor to uphold this ideal by including in our thoughts all the other students of Christian Hermeticism around the world.

We have a unique opportunity, being gathered together right now. Let us take a few minutes of quiet time to focus on this heart intention together. In the spirit that underlies *Meditations on the Tarot* it is possible to experience together what "concentration without effort" and the opening of the heart is. Let us now contemplate "listening to the beating of the world heart"—listening with our hearts at this gathering as friends of the anonymous author, to honor the spiritual path he has opened up, the path of Christian Hermeticism. We can all hold the question individually concerning the next step on the path as we endeavour to listen to the beating of the world heart.

In studying *Meditations on the Tarot* we try to understand from our level what the author means with his words, and each one of us has our own interpretation. From the first Arcanum it is clear that the starting-point is the establishing of "interior silence"—the "zone of silence." Here the author is speaking about a real experience that was for him an ever-present reality. This is no mindless silence, but a silence full of speaking. The quality of the opening exercise on the path of Christian Hermeticism is that of the listening heart and of "speaking silence." What is speaking into the silence? The author speaks of waves—of succeeding waves of silence.

What are these "waves of silence"? The actual experience of the "waves of silence" is that of communion with the being of the living Christ. However, the author does not say this expressly in words, because the moment we clothe a concept in words we conceptualize it.

Although expressed conceptually in words, the "speaking silence" is a real experience. It is an experiential level of reality as to how Christ is working in the world right now. This is true listening to the beating of the world heart—a communion with the world heart through which warmth is engendered in our own heart.

We can only find this communion through our own heart. This is the first step, the starting-point of the path of Christian initiation outlined in *Meditations on the Tarot*: true mysticism.

Step 2—Gnosis

The next step is to direct the warmth of this inner heart experience into consciousness. Our mind becomes filled with the light arising through the warmth engendered in our heart. Out of this experience, *gnosis*—inner knowing—arises.

We can also direct this warmth down from the heart into our limbs, so that we are fired to serve the *world will* through our deeds, which leads us to the next step.

Step 3—Sacred Magic

Sacred magic is when our will unites with the *divine will*. Mysticism, gnosis, and magic result from an interiorization—an individual interiorization. Each one of us has the potential to unite with the inner being of Christ and to experience Christ within. Everything Christ did on earth was done through mysticism, gnosis, and sacred magic, exactly as described in the first three Arcana. This is expressed in new language in *Meditations on the Tarot*, where the author gives indications as to how we experience mysticism, gnosis, and sacred magic in our time, opening up for us an opportunity to enter into a living relationship with Christ *here and now*. This is *the* key to working with the book *Meditations on the Tarot*.

In truth, it is more than a relationship, and more than a communion. It is a *union* with Christ within. This is what we understand by love as the key to the way of the heart. When we understand the way of the heart, then—through the heart—we move further on our path of spiritual development, becoming ever more one with the Divine.

Just now, while we were having our silent meditation, the wind was blowing. This is important in consideration of the first Arcanum, where the words quoted at the start are:

> The wind blows where it wills, and you hear the sound of it, but you do not know whence it comes or whither it goes; so it is with everyone who is born of the spirit. (John 3:8)

"The wind blows where it wills." The wind is another expression for the spirit, and the spirit always expresses itself in manifold ways. Every child brings spiritual revelation; spiritual revelation can come from the most unexpected quarter. We have to learn to be open and to go where the spirit is moving us. If we do not practise this openness, there is the danger that we can become fixed and then actually find ourselves in opposition to the living spirit.

We see examples in the life of Jesus. The most powerful force of opposition to him was that of the Pharisees, who were dedicated to the teaching of Moses. For them, this teaching was the *final word*. As far as they were concerned, Jesus was a rabble rouser from Nazareth, who dared to say that there is more than the *final word*; and they did not like hearing this.

These are seed thoughts to take in as inner nourishment for guidance and inspiration. This means that as we grow spiritually, we are able to take in more guidance for integration between our normal level of consciousness and that of our higher self. We sometimes say we have "got it" when we understand something, but there is no "getting it" in an ultimate and final sense. Rather, we have to continually move on in our spiritual growth, learning to flow with the living spirit.

Group Work

One of the questions that led to this meeting was how we might work with *Meditations on the Tarot* in a group. It is stated in the book that it is an individual endeavor. Yet there is no doubt that when we come together as a group the work deepens. If this happens in the right spirit, then the author of the work can be present, can be there helping us in the unfolding of a group process together, which is a truly enriching experience. It is on the heart level that this experience can be found.

How can we create conditions to help bring this about? What preparation is required? Are we creating the right space together, a space where the spirit underlying *Meditations on the Tarot* can enter and be present? The underlying spirit is expressed in the words: "Where two or three are gathered together in my name, there am I in the midst of them." (Matthew 18:20)

Accounts of Different Groups
Working with Meditations on the Tarot

Someone from a group in the Mid-West writes:

> Currently about ten of us meet monthly. We spend two months on each Arcanum. Our meetings are very rich experiences. The experience is deep. We meet in an environment conducive to sacred space. We gather together and spend about thirty minutes socializing. When the half hour is up we form a circle. We then sound a chime and light a candle. Then we open with sacred dance. This is quite a beautiful experience. We then seat ourselves in a circle. We invoke the presence of the Arcanum by reading the introductory verses the Unknown Author has placed for each Arcanum (except the 15th Arcanum, which does not have an opening). We then sit in silence for several minutes. At a certain point somebody speaks and then the conversation begins. An atmosphere of depth and listening prevails during the conversation.

There are several important steps each member commits to follow:

We will read the Arcanum before meeting.

We agree to link our spoken thoughts to what has just been said.

We allow silence from the end of one statement to the beginning of the next.

We are committed to the process. As the hour passes the conversation develops a flow. After an hour we stop the conversation. We end with a verse, sound the chimes and blow out the candle. All of us experience a presence during these meetings.

A Second Perspective

Here is a second perspective from a group on the West Coast that has been working with the book for many years. The participants in this group are long-standing good friends, which enables them to go to a remarkable level together. I had sent them the previous description and here is a response from one member of the group:

> There are many similarities in our approaches. Individual preparation, shared intention, creating sacred space, silence, listening, inviting the spiritual world to participate in our conversation, and reverence for the spiritual process seem to be common themes.
>
> In the past year something new has unfolded in our group. We are also active as a peace group. This has required much new learning in non-profit work and management, business processes, and financial planning. We now bring our business questions into the study group and ask for guidance to make wise decisions. We have found this to be fruitful for our questions. This allows a natural flow of energy. We continue to be moved and inspired by a loving presence and spiritual guidance.

To set this last remark in context, the writer told me that in their group they have several times had the experience, when sitting in silence, of a divine presence. This divine presence of love entered in as an experience tangible to everyone in the group. Through this common experience they have been inwardly uplifted. On one occasion the whole group was inwardly transported in a common mystical experience of divine love that lasted for about 45 minutes.

I thought it would be helpful to share the accounts of these two study groups working with *Meditations on the Tarot*. The key to the success of the study group in each case is the setting of the space and the calling in of the spiritual guide overlighting the work.

The Church of Peter & The Church of John

At the Last Supper, Peter was on the left side of Christ and John on the right. In the last chapter of the *Gospel of John* there is a conversation where the Risen One asks Peter three times: "Do you love me?" Each time Peter replies affirmatively. Then Christ says: "Feed my sheep."

This means that Peter (and thereby to the Church of Peter) is given the task of administering the sacraments until the end of time. Peter then turns around and—seeing John—asks, "What about him?" The Risen One replies, "If it is my will that he shall wait until I come again, what is that to you?" (John 21:21–22)

What is indicated by this conversation? John (and thereby the Church of John) is holding something until the time of the Second Coming—the esoteric dimension, the heights and the depths of Christ's teaching.

What happened when Christianity was founded? The exoteric Church of Peter and the esoteric Church of John were initially one. However, with the spread of Christianity, the teaching spread in the widths but lost the dimension of the heights and the depths.

John is to hold the dimension of the heights and depths through the course of history until the time comes when the deeper teaching can flow back into the outer form of Christianity, reunifying the exoteric and esoteric, bringing true religion by restoring this missing dimension. It is through this that reunion with the Divine takes place.

This is alluded to briefly in the first Arcanum. The task of Christianity through the sacraments (Church of Peter) leads the individual to the threshold of the divine spiritual realm. The task of the Church of John is to take the next step across the threshold through the meeting with Christ and the great initiation. Through working with *Meditations on the Tarot* we are able to connect with the stream of John.

It is important to realize that the work of Peter and that of John are complementary, that they are not opposed. Through the work of the Church of John it is possible to experience the liturgy and communion *within consciousness*, that is, to come into a communion experience within the sphere of our own consciousness. The holy sacrament is translated to an *inner, interior experience*. Within the Church of Peter the liturgy or mass is celebrated. The work of the Church of John does not replace the mass. We are all learning and are at different stages, and even when the holy sacrament has become an inner experience of consciousness, the celebration of the mass still has relevance for countless people in the world, who are experiencing and learning something through it. It is all part of the evolution of Christianity, where human beings are allowed to grow in the work of Christ in creating the New Jerusalem. This is the work we are called to do through the path of Christian Hermeticism.

Egyptian Mysteries

Let us try now to understand what Christian Hermeticism is. Why "Hermeticism?" This word signifies a connection with the stream of the Egyptian mysteries. When one enters into the experience of the Egyptian mysteries one discovers that the whole life of the people of ancient Egypt was focused on the life after death—on the encounter with the afterlife, when the soul was weighed in the judgment hall of Osiris. Knowledge of this was transmitted in the Egyptian priesthood at different mystery centers.

The priests were supposed to cross, during life, the threshold of death. Even while in the physical body the initiate could be aware of what takes place in the afterlife, and it was through such experiences that the text central to the Egyptian priesthood—*The Egyptian Book of the Dead*—was written.

Such knowledge is implicit in the words of the author of *Meditations on the Tarot*, who in his introduction greets us from "beyond the grave," referring to the realm beyond life. He was able to write this book because in his earthly life he had already crossed the threshold of death on the level of consciousness. What he sets forth as the path of Christian Hermeticism is not so much a matter of accumulating knowledge, but is primarily one of moral development. That is the main criterion. We have to make ourselves inwardly morally mature enough and then we will be able to cross this threshold already in earthly life. We are all going to cross it at the time of death, but we can—like the ancient Egyptian priest-initiates—cross it already in life.

Raising of Lazarus

The greatest example of a threshold experience manifested in the life of Christ is the raising of Lazarus. This was the first time in humankind's history where the nature of initiation (previously a temple secret) was shown publicly.

The Pharisees were shocked and said that this was a breach; but they had other motivations for their hostility toward Jesus (the initiator) and Lazarus (the initiated one) as well.

The raising of Lazarus from the dead was an archetypal metamorphosis of the initiation of the ancient Egyptian mysteries. Lazarus had crossed the threshold. The book *Jesus, Lazarus and the Messiah: Three Christian Mysteries* (by Charles Tidball and myself) gives an account of who Lazarus was. This great Christian initiate was the writer of the *Gospel of John* and Revelation. What shines through the Christian initiation he underwent is a metamorphosis of the initiation undergone in the ancient Egyptian mysteries.

The anonymous author has brought us into connection with a mystery tradition that goes back thousands of years—the great mystery stream borne by the pharaohs and priests of ancient Egypt. This latter went through a metamorphosis with the coming of Christ, and is now presented to us in a new form in the book *Meditations on the Tarot*. This metamorphosis concerns the threshold experience between life and death, and how to arrive at it through moral evolution.

Each Arcanum is a teaching intended to initiate us into what is needed to transform ourselves into moral beings. The primary truth expressed by the new initiation is that it is accomplished through moral evolution. It is only then—through moral evolution—that we become fully human beings. The drama happening in the world at the present time is a lesson. The drama is that human beings are assenting to something degenerate, something leading human beings to become "asses," as it is put in the *Srimad Bhagavatam*, when predicting the coming of the Kalki Avatar. In this process of degeneration the influence of the mass media cannot be underestimated.

As human beings we are *homo sapiens* (Latin *sapientia* = wisdom = Sophia). Human beings are called to be a family of wise beings—beings who do not just acquire knowledge, but become moral. This is what the work with *Meditations on the Tarot* is really about. You can read it, meditate on it, and keep discovering thereby ever new levels on the path of Christian Hermeticism, because there is no end to the unfolding of divine love within us from one level to the next.

In an evolutionary sense we are approaching ever nearer to the heart of God, which is Love. This—as an archetype—underlies the mystery of the Ascension, which took place forty days after Christ told Mary Magdalene in the Garden of the Holy Sepulcher early on Easter Sunday morning that He would soon depart: "I am ascending to the Father." (John 20:17)

Forty days later, in the hours preceding the Ascension, the disciples were gathered with the Virgin Mary in the hall of the Last

Supper. They were joined by the Risen One, whom they beheld, and who then guided them through the streets of Jerusalem to the Mount of Olives. Ascending the mount together, they beheld the Risen One becoming more and more radiant with light.

They arrived with the Risen One at the summit of the Mount of Olives and there beheld Him dissolve into a radiant cloud of supernatural light. Above Him they saw a rainbow, and two Angels appeared and spoke to the disciples, saying: "Ye men of Galilee, why do you stand looking up to heaven? This Jesus, who was taken up from you into heaven, will come again in the same way as you have seen him ascend." (Acts 1:11)

"He will come in the clouds" (Rev. 1:7)—not in the physical body, but as a presence (Greek *parousia*). This *divine presence* is an actual human being who has gone through death, conquered it through resurrection, ascended to the heights, and returned. And it is union and communion with this being, with this *divine presence*, that is at the heart of the spiritual practice outlined in the first Arcanum of *Meditations on the Tarot*. At each level of His ascent through the spiritual hierarchies—Angels, Archangels, Archai, Exusiai, Dynamis, Kyriotetes, Thrones, Cherubim, Seraphim— He taught and brought something into that realm. He revealed to the spiritual hierarchies what He had accomplished in overcoming death.

This was the beginning of a new creation: the creation of a new heaven. Now we are living in the time of His return, that of the Second Coming, a new era of activity of Christ for which the book *Meditations on the Tarot* is a preparation. Christ is present insofar as we allow Him to work through us through mysticism, gnosis, and sacred magic. In this way we participate in the spiritualization of the earth that will come together and unite with the new heaven in the creation of the New Jerusalem.

In conclusion, one further aspect should be mentioned, which will help bring another dimension to our work with *Meditations on the Tarot*. The West—and that includes the English-speaking people of the British Isles and this continent of North America—has as

20

its central spiritual archetype the *Grail quest*. This is the first Arcanum: the *Arcanum of the Holy Grail*. What is the Holy Grail? It is the experience of *silent communion* with Christ. The key to the Grail story is that each individual in the story was at his or her appointed position in order to bear a particular aspect of the being of Christ at that time.

It was a path of *interior silence* to allow the soul to become a Grail vessel into which the spirit is poured. This is the essence of the first Arcanum: that we become Grail vessels. Our gathering today was a coming together to bring to consciousness the nature of the path of Christian Hermeticism, which is a modern form of the Grail quest that leads to the great initiation through Christ.

II

Hermeticism Lecture
2007

This is the second annual meeting on Christian Hermeticism, focusing on the book *Meditations on the Tarot*, which was completed exactly forty years ago. If you turn to the end of the book you will see that the date of completion is May 21, 1967—although it was not published until many years later. The first French edition appeared in 1980, thirteen years after the book was completed, and the English translation was first published in 1985.

Shortly after Christmas 1977, I was invited to Amsterdam. The person with whom I had corresponded about *Meditations on the Tarot* gave me the French manuscript and told me that I was the person to translate it into English. That is how the manuscript came into my hands.

I took this work seriously, translating the manuscript during the four years (1978–1982), when I was in Switzerland studying eurythmy. I also spent much time in the library of the British Museum researching the many quotations. I finished the translation of the whole manuscript in 1982 and then sent it to somebody who on my behalf looked for a publisher. The English translation was finally published in 1985.

During the work of translating the manuscript I received continual help and guidance. That is how I came to know and experience the truth of the words written by the author in his Foreword to *Meditations on the Tarot*: "The reader will know the author better through the Letters [on the major Arcana of the Tarot] than through any other source." For me this was—and still is—the most astounding thing: it is a work that is magical. The moment we start working with it we come into connection with the author, who is able to answer our questions. This is a priceless treasure. It is a magical book that you can read again and again. Many people I know work with the book by using it to answer their questions and problems. They open the book and on the page to which they open they find the answers.

Why the French Language?

In a private conversation the author described the task of writing *Meditations on the Tarot* as a "commission" from the spiritual world, part of which was to write the book in French. Moreover, as he points out in the Foreword, in France there already existed a extensive literature on the Tarot.

In 1781 the French Egyptologist and esotericist Court de Gebelin published a work on the Tarot, stating that the Tarot was the lost Book of Hermes or Thoth from ancient Egypt and contained all the ancient Egyptian mystery wisdom. That stimulated a tremendous interest in this game of cards—the Tarot. This is why such a voluminous literature (several thousand books) exists on

Count of St. Germain

the Tarot or on Tarot-related subjects in France. (It is worth noting that the Tarot as a game of cards was not known before the fifteenth century. The first recorded mention of Tarot cards was in 1442 at the Court of Ferrara in Italy.)

However, there is obviously a deeper reason why it was written in French. When you read the text you can see that the author is forging a connection with a particular spiritual stream: that of the French esotericists—including Court de Gebelin, Fabre d'Olivet, Papus, Eliphas Lévi, Saint-Yves d'Alveydre, and Maître Philippe— which goes back to the figure of the Count of St. Germain (1696– 1784), who is considered (at least in the West) to be humanity's leading spiritual teacher. The work of Court de Gebelin started the wave of interest in the Tarot as a book of Egyptian mystery wisdom. His book was published toward the end of the life of the Count de Saint Germain, who no doubt was a source of inspiration for Court de Gebelin's work.

The task of *Meditations on the Tarot* is to bring the ancient Egyptian mystery wisdom over into a Christianized form, and this helps to understand something of the background as to why it was written in French, which of course made it possible to connect with the spiritual stream inaugurated in France by the Count of St. Germain. There are other reasons why the French language was chosen. For example, it is a language that formulates concepts in a very clear way, making it suitable for the transmission of mystery wisdom, which is partly why in France a great wave of esotericism followed in the wake of the incarnation of the Count of St. Germain.

Path of Christian Initiation

There are several levels on which we can approach *Meditations on the Tarot*. A major key is offered when we consider that it is a testament from a great spiritual teacher—as indicated at our meeting in 2006—who reveals himself in the first Arcanum as being connected with the stream of John. He reveals also that the stream of John is working together with the stream of Peter, rather than in opposition to it. One of the distinguishing features of *Meditations on the Tarot* is that it is a work of Christian esotericism that is not opposed to traditional Christianity; rather, it tries to build a bridge between the esoteric stream represented by John and the exoteric stream represented by Peter. This is a very important point and has a deep esoteric background.

Another key to approaching this work is to immerse oneself in it as a book of initiation, a book offered to each person who will work with it meditatively as a path of Christian initiation. This aspect is also made evident in the first Arcanum, where it is clearly stated that the goal is the *great initiation*, which is the initiation through Christ himself.

Meditations on the Tarot is an expression of what is called the Christ School, which exists as a spiritual reality. The point of entry into this School is found in the words of St. Paul, "Not I, but Christ in me." (Galatians 2:20) We could express this more simply as "Christ in me." It is a matter of bringing to expression as far as possible the Christ Consciousness within oneself. This is the goal of *Meditations on the Tarot*. And those who are part of this Christ School are those who have brought "Christ in me" to some degree of realization.

The author of *Meditations on the Tarot* is one who has accomplished this to a very high degree. On this account, he can write authoritatively about the steps we need to take to enter into the Christ School, which is above all a path of moral evolution, or moral development, and not so much one of acquiring esoteric knowledge—at least, not first and foremost. Rather, it is a matter of entering the School of Christ through *moral deepening*, and this is what shines through every sentence in *Meditations on the Tarot*.

Symbols

Let us consider the extensive use of symbols in the book. One can approach symbols in the sense of Carl Gustav Jung, who indicated that they express great archetypes. To clarify what is meant by this, we need to understand that there are *spiritual archetypes*. For example, if we look up to the starry heavens, we see the different constellations. We might see, for example, the constellation of Orion, which is one of the most well known. For the ancient Egyptians, Orion was seen as an image in the heavens of Osiris—the central god for the Egyptian religion. For them, looking up to Orion was an experience of the being of Osiris.

This is what we could call a cosmic archetype. When we look more closely at the constellation of Orion we see that the stars are positioned in a certain pattern (discussed in the eighteenth

Arcanum, "the Moon"). It is the pattern of the Tree of Life. Thus, when we look at the image of the Tree of Life, we find more or less the same image as when we look at the constellation of Orion. The archetype may appear in the heavens and also in human consciousness. For the Egyptians it appeared in the heavens. For the teachers and students of the Jewish esoteric tradition known as the Kabbalah it appeared in consciousness. The Tree of Life is central to the whole of the Jewish esoteric tradition of the Kabbalah. Various spiritual teachers have spoken about this significant image.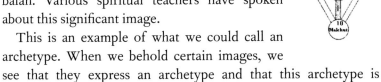

This is an example of what we could call an archetype. When we behold certain images, we see that they express an archetype and that this archetype is brought into relationship with the soul. Then it is no longer an abstract pattern. It speaks on the level of the soul. In the Tarot symbols, cosmic archetypes are brought down to the language of the soul in pictures. Our task is to explore them and to deepen into each image in order to find the cosmic archetype underlying each.

Fairy tales also work with images that express cosmic archetypes. For instance, Sleeping Beauty waits for the Prince to come and awaken her with a kiss. Sleeping Beauty is a symbol for the human soul—the soul waiting to be awakened by the Prince, or the Higher Self. If we wish to understand what is being communicated in fairy tales, we have to learn to understand the language of archetypes expressed in symbols, which is also the language of the soul. Those who have studied Jung will understand the importance of this in the field of psychology.

Tarot: *The Lost Book of Thoth*

What distinguishes the images in the Tarot, as Court de Gebelin proposed, is that they comprise the lost Book of Thoth. The esotericist Rudolf Steiner also spoke of the Tarot as the lost Book of

Thoth, or the lost Book of Hermes (identifying Hermes with Thoth). This means that we have to do here with images, carried  over from the ancient Egyptian mystery tradition, that have resurfaced in a metamorphosed way in our time. In other words, the Tarot is a spiritual path, and the Tarot images have been carried over from the mysteries of ancient Egypt. They are authentic symbols, each image expressing the essence of a stage on the path of initiation as practiced in ancient Egypt.

But considering the thousands of books written on the Tarot, why are we focusing on this one book, *Meditations on the Tarot*?

Finding the right interpretation of the Tarot images requires a high level of consciousness and morality capable of penetrating the symbols in the right way. This is what is unique about *Meditations on the Tarot*. I cannot speak about all the other books on the Tarot, since I have not read all of this extensive literature. What can be said about *Meditations on the Tarot*, however, is that it has the stamp of a master speaking through the words and images.

The method followed by the author of *Meditations on the Tarot* was something he developed in his preliminary studies of the images of Tarot cards. This methodology has now been revealed through the inclusion of material published in this volume for the first time in English translation (see Part II). This material comprises notes made by the author of *Meditations on the Tarot*. These were his preparatory notes before writing the book—and these reveal his method. Unfortunately, the notes cover only the last nine Arcana, from XIV to XXII. The notes to the first thirteen Arcana have gone missing.

The Star—Arcanum XVII

There are many different Tarot images, among them those from the Tarot of Marseilles. As far as the author of *Meditations on*

the *Tarot* is concerned, the images from the Tarot of Marseilles are authentic. And it is evident that images from other Tarot decks have often been so worked over that they are sometimes hardly recognizable as Tarot images anymore. The author's meditations are therefore focused upon the images from the Tarot of Marseilles.

With each Arcanum—in this example we shall be looking at Arcanum XVII, "the Star"—the author goes through five steps. I will enumerate these five steps so that we can apply the same approach to each Arcanum for ourselves. To give some background to these steps, he refers to the *mystical* meaning of each card, the *gnostic* meaning, the *magical* meaning, and the *philosophical* meaning. We are familiar with these four levels of meaning already from the first four Arcana of *Meditations on the Tarot*, where the first is the Arcanum of mysticism, the second that of gnosis, the third that of sacred magic, and the fourth the hermetic-philosophical Arcanum. With these first four Arcana we already have the outline of the method; but then in addition the author indicates a fifth step, which is the *esoteric* meaning. The esoteric meaning is a synthesis of the first four.

Layout of the Card

When we are contemplating a particular Arcanum, such as the Star, there is first the layout of the card. This context is given in relation to the preceding card; it is like a journey from image to image through all twenty-two Arcana.

The layout of the card we are now going to focus on—the Star—stands in relation to the preceding one, Arcanum XVI, the Tower of Destruction. The author refers to this latter as the Arcanum of Decadence. When something becomes decadent, it is Divine Law that it be destroyed. We see this with the cities of

Sodom and Gomorrah, which had grown totally decadent and were destroyed by a blast or some kind of natural catastrophe on an enormous scale. The image of lightning striking and destroying the tower is an expression of what happens in the case of decadence, and this is the image we see in Arcanum XVI, the Tower of Destruction.

After the Arcanum of Decadence comes that of re-establishing. There is destruction, represented by the Tower of Destruction, and then this is followed by the principle of re-establishment. That is the Divine Law. In the published notes, here are the author's words relating to this: "The stars, through the intermediary of the true (naked) feminine, render earthly life fruitful" (see image on preceding page). The re-establishing comes from the higher world, the world of stars. It is the feminine principle that is able to nurture and re-establish earthly life. This is portrayed in Arcanum XVII, the Star, by the image of the star above; and we also see the representative of the feminine, kneeling and pouring out the water that renders earthly life fruitful.

General Meaning

The author elucidates the layout of each Arcanum and then comes to the general meaning. Here are the notes for Arcanum XVII (The Star):

The general meaning of this Arcanum:

The unconscious (in the sense of C. G. Jung) unites the consciousness (the "Day") of the human being with the starry world. In this way the aridity (fatigue, sterility, senility) of terrestrial life (day consciousness) is rendered fertile in the silence of the "nocturnal" realms of consciousness or in sleep. The liquid that nourishes— keeps alive—the soul is *Hope*.

For this reason he refers to this card as the *Arcanum of Hope*.

The woman depicted in the image of Arcanum XVII represents hope. As we know from Christian theology, hope is one of the three cardinal virtues (faith, hope, and love). Hope is an important esoteric principle. We must never give up hope. Hope is what nourishes the soul. However gloomy things might look, we must keep alive the flame of hope.

However, modern life is largely oriented toward creating a sense of hopelessness—for example, through creating the illusion that we are predetermined through our genes, and in other ways as well. The author, in his notes, goes on to look at some of these ways.

Astrology

Astrology is one area where there is a tendency to regard the human being as predetermined. The author states: "*Soul astrology*—as the wisdom of Hope." And he quotes St. Thomas: *Astra inclinant, non necessitant* [The stars incline, they do not compel].

This teaching is intrinsic to soul astrology. From studying a horoscope it is possible to see tendencies. Soul astrology shows tendencies, but it is not compelling.

In this context the author refers to the "eighth planet" in the horoscope, which is the concrete hope present in every stellar configuration (over and above the seven classical planets according to which the days of the week are named: Saturn, Sun, Moon, Mars, Mercury, Jupiter, Venus).

Often an astrologer, looking at some planetary configuration in a horoscope, might say that it looks bad or even ominous. In fact, however, there is hope in every configuration; it is always present.

Karma

After discussing astrology as a subject where the human being is subject to belief in predetermination, the author points to the transcendental self and refers to *dharma* in the domain of *karma*. My understanding is that *dharma* is what the human being attains by way of grace that goes beyond *karma*. With *karma* we are obliged to make good our transgressions from the past. But *dharma* is the law of grace that operates beyond the level of *karma*. Here, too, there is hope, which counterbalances the sense of predetermination through being subject to *karma*.

The great spiritual teachers are those who have to a large extent overcome negative *karma* and are living more in the sense of *dharma*. In other words they are really free.

Heredity

After astrology and *karma* (viewed together as being interrelated) the second area explored by the author is concerned with heredity. Here we are conditioned to think of ourselves as being preconditioned through our genes. From the author's notes we read:

> Heredity—seen in the day of the wisdom of Hope: the "eighth planet" in the hereditary constellation. *Hereditas inclinat, non necessitant* [Heredity inclines, it does not compel].

Health

The third area considered by the author relates to health and concerns the contemporary medical view of the human being. According to predetermination in the realm of health, it is clear that in the contemporary medical-biological perspective we are also predetermined. We have our "bank account" of health and illness and we just have to live with it. Quoting again from the author's notes:

> *Health (medicine)*—seen through the wisdom of Hope: the "eighth planet" in the constellation, that is, the "humors" (hormones) and glands. *Glandulae inclinant, non necessitant* [The glands incline, they do not compel].

Occult Physiology

After astrology and karma, heredity, and health and illness, the fourth area addressed by the author is predetermination according to the "occult physiology" of *Nephesh* and *Ruach*. These terms are from the Kabbalah and are Hebrew expressions. *Nephesh* is the life force and *Ruach* is the soul.

Occult (esoteric) physiology has to do with the seven chakras as the soul organs of the human being. Here the author points out that the chakras or lotus flowers "incline, they do not compel."

He speaks of the "eighth lotus." This is something beyond the seven lotus flowers, an unknown element, and this is what gives hope. The faculty or virtue of hope gradually opens up for us. It is above all nourishment: in the image of Arcanum XVII we see the woman pouring out that which is nourishing for the soul. We can see this force working on different levels from above downward. From the level of "I" consciousness hope works down into the level of the soul, and from there it pours down into the life forces, and from this level it works down further into the physical. If we learn to acquire mastery in practicing this Arcanum, there will be a continual nourishing flow of hope, positivity, and optimism that can open up tremendous possibilities in life.

Each and every Arcanum mirrors a great spiritual archetype and embodies a principle of initiation. If we could bring just one Arcanum to realization, this would transform our lives. Just by meditating on the image we start to activate this Arcanum in the depths of the subconscious and it begins to work.

The images speak on a soul level and activate the soul. They are a *fertilizing* element. You can experience this if you show them to somebody who has never seen these images before, laying them out one by one. Generally people will find that one Tarot card really speaks to them. It may be that most of the Tarot cards do not say much, but then one particular card suddenly opens up something profoundly meaningful because that is what is occupying them on a subconscious level. That could be a way of working with the cards in the field of psychotherapy. A way of finding someone's soul problem at a particular time would be to take note of their response to the images of the various Arcana at that time.

Predestination in Theology

After illuminating the area of occult physiology, which has to do with the lotus flowers, the fifth realm considered by the author is that of predestination in theology. Calvin brought forward the idea that we are all predestined, that some are predestined to arrive in the Heavenly Jerusalem and some are not. This is based on the idea of the 144,000 chosen ones.

Reading now from the author's notes:

> To be "chosen" or "condemned" (predestination) in Theology:
> Good and evil incline, they do not compel.

One could lose hope if everything truly were predestined on a theological level.

The author then quotes various sayings from Catholic tradition relating to the Virgin Mary. She is the salvation of the sick, the refuge of sinners, the consoler of the afflicted; and later (see below) he gives the meaning of the mystical mantle of the Virgin.

Continuing to quote from the author's notes:

> *Gratia gratis data: Malum et Bonum inclinant, non necessitant—*
> *nulla praedestinatio, sed spec omnibus* [Grace given gratuitously:
> Good and evil incline, they do not compel—no predestination, but
> hope for all].

This is a wonderful message. Even if somebody has hit rock bottom in life, there is still hope.

Reading now the author's summary:

> The XVIIth Arcanum refutes *determinism* in all domains—
> astrology, heredity, physiology, inner karmic constellation, and
> theology; it offers grounds for *Hope*. It is the VIIIth repeated: Jus-
> tice includes grace, Hope.

There is an application of numerology here: $1 + 7 = 8 =$ "eighth planet"; and the eighth Arcanum is Justice. So far the author's notes have indicated the general meaning of the seventeenth Arcanum, and now follows the specific meaning.

Mystical Meaning

When we contemplate the image of the feminine being, this nourishing feminine being of the seventeenth Arcanum, we experience that she is surrounded by stars. This is her starry mantle, upon which we can always call. It is a symbol of hope. But it is more than a symbol; the starry mantle of the Mother is an actual spiritual reality.

Let us try to reach back to the Egyptian mysteries. Each of the Tarot cards is carrying something over from ancient Egypt, from the ancient mysteries. When the Egyptians looked up to the stars, they saw the whole starry heavens as the mantle of Isis. We see here in this Arcanum how this experience is carried over from the Egyptian mysteries. But now, instead of Isis, it is related to the starry mantle of the Virgin Mary. That is the mystical meaning of this Arcanum.

Gnostic Meaning

The gnostic meaning—the second level—is that of the world intercessor: Ave (or Eva = Eve), Sophia, Mary, Virgin, Queen, Mother. This gnostic meaning brings us back to the World Soul— Sophia—who is the World Intercessor.

Let us pause a moment to reflect on this. In approaching these spiritual archetypes, it is difficult to have access to them in a direct and immediate way, unless we are at a very advanced level of development. However, through the World Soul, Sophia, we are able to experience a reflection of the archetype, which we are then able to enter into and take in.

Let me illustrate this with an example: that of the three magi. In *Meditations on the Tarot* the author speaks of the three magi in the nineteenth Arcanum, in relation to "following one's star." The magi were able to read directly from the stars in the heavens; they could access the spiritual archetypes. They were initiates, and thus were able to discern from the stars that the birth of the Messiah had taken place.

Let us contrast the three magi, who read the spiritual archetypes directly, with the sixteenth-century French prophet Nostradamus, who made his prophecies using a bowl of water. This bowl was positioned in such a way that it would reflect the stars. At night he would look into the bowl and read from the reflection. This is analogous to the World Soul, which reflects the great spiritual archetypes.

In fact, the whole earth does reflect the heavens, and this reflection is something we can read in the book of nature. Nature is much closer to us, and so reading it is more direct than trying to read from the starry heavens. That is one way of interpreting the gnostic meaning of the seventeenth Arcanum.

Moreover, the whole set of Tarot cards comprises a path on which spiritual archetypes may be read on a soul level.

Magical Meaning

This has to do with "magical medicine." One aspect of *magical medicine* is

> the use by the Mage ("eighth planet") of the *healing* forces of the 7 planets; the use of the *great cosmic pharmacy* by the magician-doctor, the magician-pharmacist, and the magician-nurse.

Following these words the author gives the example of using mantras for healing. What he is pointing to is a principle for the future—to be able to work with mantras in a healing way. When someone goes to a medical doctor in the future, we can envisage that the doctor will diagnose their problem and will be able to give them a healing mantram which, if they repeat it over and over, will heal them.

Philosophical Meaning

Then comes the philosophical meaning of the seventeenth Arcanum. In *Meditations on the Tarot* the author refers to this in the context of the fourth Arcanum, where he uses the expression "hermetic-philosophical." Reading his notes on Arcanum XVII:

> *The philosophy and medicine*: holism—the world as an organic whole, the human being as an organic whole; *vis mediatrix naturae* [the healing power of nature].

In our time we are coming increasingly to see things holistically; not just diagnosing and trying to treat a part, but considering the whole organism and treating the problem accordingly. According to the author's notes, this has to do with

> the methods of knowledge of the truth, of perfecting oneself morally, of the expiation of sins, and of the re-establishment of health.

All of this has to do with the principle of health and illness. If we are ill, we seek to re-establish health. Philosophically speaking, if we want to re-establish health, we need to find knowledge of the truth. We need to follow the path of perfecting ourselves morally, and also redeem what has taken place in the past.

Esoteric Meaning

Lastly, the esoteric meaning of the seventeenth Arcanum is that of a universal remedy or panacea—which means "all remedy."

> *Medicina universalis*—the universal remedy (panacea): the *ensouled Word* (Logos *and* Sophia—*through* Sophia) moving the seven healing forces of the planets.

Here the author is alluding to healing through union with the Word. The stages of this healing are, he says,

> truth, consolation, peace, joy—(accepting the truth, consolation through the truth, peace resulting from complete consolation, and joy resulting from the peace). . . .

In the notes we also read that this is

> the healing mystery of the Night (the super-consciousness).
>
> The Night of Christmas: the Word is born solely *in* and *through* the Virgin; it is the same in the individual inner life.

This is a very interesting point, that the birth of Christ takes place within us through the Sophia or through the Divine Feminine. As a final comment he speaks of the impoverishment caused by Protestantism, which by and large abandoned the Feminine.

> [W]ithout the Mother the Word is not ensouled, and consequently humanity is deprived of the effect of the *Universal Remedy*.

Here he is referring to Christ as the "Universal Remedy," which is accessed through Sophia or the Feminine represented in the image of the seventeenth Arcanum (and other Tarot images as well). This is one aspect of the Divine Feminine.

If the Word is not ensouled by the Feminine,

> humanity is deprived of the effect of the *Universal Remedy*. Christ becomes a Master who only *teaches*, not a Universal Healer.

More and more the tendency is to look upon Christ as the Great Teacher. In fact, everywhere he went, Christ taught *and* healed. The first miracle of the *Gospel of St. John*, the wedding at Cana, indicates this very clearly. There the miraculous deeds of the Son were born through the Mother. At the wedding feast, the miracle of the transformation of water into wine took place. The Virgin Mary was present at the wedding feast and it was she who said to Jesus there: "It is your turn to provide the wine." At this juncture the Bible is usually translated incorrectly. Christ reportedly said "What does this have to do with thee, woman?" A more correct translation from the Greek would read, "What is it that weaves between you and me, woman?"

This is an expression of Christ working together with the Divine Feminine; and through this the miracle was able to take place.

Summary

What we have considered above gives some indication of the approach of the author to penetrating the mystery of each Arcanum. To summarize:

(1)There is first the context of the card. Which Arcanum does it follow? What is its place in the whole sequence of Arcana?

(2)There is the general meaning of the Arcanum, as revealed by the image expressing it.

(3)There are specific meanings—the mystical, gnostic, magical, philosophical, and esoteric meanings.

This summarizes the path of approach the author followed for each Arcanum, and this method can be very helpful for us in our own efforts to penetrate to the deeper levels of the Arcana.

We have considered this approach in relation to the seventeenth Arcanum, and now that the author's notes are being published, we can study this approach also for Arcana XIV–XXII. Apart from the inherent interest of the content of his remarks on Arcana XIV–XXII specifically, the notes reveal further aspects of his methodological approach.

With regard to meditation, the most powerful approach is to choose a particular Arcanum and then go through the different stages enumerated above: mystical, gnostic, magical, philosophical, and esoteric. In this way we can identify ourselves with it: we can "step into" it. For example, in relation to Arcanum XVII, through identification one "becomes" the feminine being who is depicted on this card as nurturing—thus entering into an experience of the star or stars that she is mediating from the starry heavens above.

However, there is one Arcanum where this approach is not to be recommended. The only Tarot image we should not identify with is the fifteenth—the Devil. The author indicates in *Meditations on the Tarot* that we must not identify with the principle of evil, for it can wreak havoc. It is a fact that even by thinking about something we attract it. It is better to think about Good rather than Evil, and to look to the future with hope.

I would like to close by reading the following from Arcanum XVII, the Arcanum of Hope:

> The message of the woman kneeling under the stars on the bank of a current which flows from the past into the future—a woman who never ceases to pour water from above into the flow of water below. It is she who is the mother of the future, and this is why her message confronts us with duty towards the future—the duty towards the flow of uninterrupted tradition.

III

Hermeticism Lecture
2008

Introduction

The anonymous author of *Meditations on the Tarot: A Journey into Christian Hermeticism* writes in his Foreword:

> These Letters on the twenty-two Major Arcana of the Tarot represent, in essence, twenty-two spiritual exercises by means of which you, dear Unknown Friend, will immerse yourself in the current of the living tradition. . . .

Another spiritual teacher of the twentieth century who contributed to this living tradition was Rudolf Steiner, who spoke thus of the Tarot as the "Book of Thoth":

> The Book of Thoth by the Egyptians consisted of 78 cards, which contained the world secrets. This was well known in the initiation rituals of Egypt. . . . Those who were initiated in the Egyptian Mysteries were able to read the symbol for Tarot. They could also read the Book of Thoth, which comprised 78 cards in which all world events were depicted from the beginning to the end, from Alpha to Omega, which one could decipher if they were arranged in their proper order. The book contained pictures of life, leading to death, and arising again to new life. Whoever could combine the correct numbers with the correct pictures could read what was written. . . .[1]

---

1. Rudolf Steiner, *The Misraim Service* (Gt. Barrington, MA: SteinerBooks, 2006), p375 — the symbol for Tarot is reproduced on this page and later in this lecture.

Hermeticism Lecture 2008

At today's meeting—this one in 2008 being our third yearly meeting—we will focus on the relationship between the Hermetic tradition represented by the author of *Meditations on the Tarot: A Journey into Christian Hermeticism* and the contribution to this tradition made by Rudolf Steiner. In exploring this relationship we will discover a wonderful and fructifying symbiosis. For example, the symbol of the Tarot indicated by Rudolf Steiner offers a profound point of departure for grasping the spiritual path offered in *Meditations on the Tarot*.

All of us here at this meeting are working with *Meditations on the Tarot* in a serious and dedicated way. As you know, the book was written during the years 1960 to 1967, and the author dates the completion of the manuscript to May 21, 1967. Now, forty-one years later, the readership of this spiritual classic numbers many thousands and it has been translated not only from French into English, but also into German, Italian, Spanish, Portuguese, and Russian. As shown by our two previous meetings here in Petaluma in 2006 and 2007, interest exists—at least for a number of students of Christian Hermeticism—to meet and share the fruits of experiences on this spiritual path.

There are people working with *Meditations on the Tarot* in many different countries. As translator of this book I have experienced over and over again people coming to express their gratitude to me for translating this work. Moreover, many express how this book has changed their lives. That alone tells us something about this work that puts it in another category than the normal type of book.

What is presented right away in the author's Foreword to the book is that he is addressing us from "beyond the grave." This means, when you start working with this book, that you enter into a relationship with a being who is no longer living on the earth, who wrote this work well aware that people would later take it up as a spiritual schooling at a time when he would be able to guide the reader from spiritual realms. He describes it as a spiritual schooling through the twenty-two meditations it contained. He is a spiritual guide from the world beyond who accompanies us in our study of this work. That is a second reason that makes this a very unique book.

If one were to characterize the tradition in which this book finds its place, it would be that of the Egyptian mysteries. These mysteries are presented in a new form. We could speak of a "resurrection" of the Egyptian mysteries, and this resurrection is through Christ, who is introduced in the first chapter as the Master on this spiritual path of Christian Hermeticism.

In the very first Letter (or Arcanum) of *Meditations on the Tarot*, that of "The Magician," reference is made to the great initiation, and that this initiation is through the Master, through meeting with the Master; and also that this encounter is of eternal value, which expresses the true value of this book. To set the encounter with the Master in context, it is evident that there is a parallel between the twenty-two Major Arcana of the Tarot and the twenty-two chapters of Revelation. The encounter with the Master described in the first chapter of Revelation was a meeting of John on the Isle of Patmos with his Initiator, who showed him the mysteries of the future. This—or something similar—is what is referred to in the first Arcanum of *Meditations on the Tarot* as the great initiation, which can best be understood through the parallel between the first Arcanum and the first chapter of Revelation. When reference is made to the meeting with the Master, the great initiation, this is exactly what is spoken of in the first chapter of Revelation. Therefore, in terms of setting *Meditations on the Tarot* in the context of a spiritual stream: it is on the one hand a resurrection of the Egyptian mystery stream, and on the other hand it is also an expression of the Johannine stream as revealed in Revelation.

Those who take up this book and begin to study it and to immerse themselves in it will have the experience of coming into an atmosphere of a profoundly loving presence. This is the experience of connecting with the Johannine stream. It is a profound and loving presence that one experiences in the moments of silence alluded to in the first Arcanum in connection with the practice of "concentration without effort." There this is described as "listening to the beating of the world heart." One learns to connect through one's own heart with the beating of the world heart.

Today our special focus, however, is the relationship of *Meditations on the Tarot* with the work of Rudolf Steiner. Many of you will know that Rudolf Steiner was a great spiritual teacher active in the first quarter of the twentieth century who left to humanity a vast legacy of books and lectures that contain profound wisdom.

What distinguishes Rudolf Steiner from most other spiritual teachers was that he was able to bring his spiritual knowledge into practical manifestation. He pioneered a new form of pedagogy known as Waldorf education. He also introduced a new form of medicine (anthroposophical medicine), new forms of art, drama, recitation, and also eurythmy, a new art of movement, as well as pioneering many other areas.

Those familiar with the work of Rudolf Steiner know that his life was one of service dedicated to bringing new spiritual knowledge to humanity in the twentieth century, to humankind entering into the modern secular age—a time when more and more, through science and technology, its connection to spiritual realms was rapidly disappearing.

What we shall focus on today is the way the spiritual path outlined in *Meditations on the Tarot* complements the spiritual path described by Rudolf Steiner. With respect to the Tarot, the first mention of this theme by Rudolf Steiner was in a lecture he held in his first esoteric school on December 12, 1906.[1] In this brief reference he refers to the Tarot under the name of the *Book of Thoth*.

Before turning our attention to this, it is important to know that back in the eighteenth century, in the year 1781, the French esotericist and Egyptologist Court de Gébelin put forward that the Tarot

---

1. In 1902 Rudolf Steiner became general secretary of the Theosophical Society in Germany and in 1904 he assumed leadership of the esoteric school within the German Theosophical Society. This esoteric school continued for ten years until the outbreak of World War I in 1914. Shortly before Rudolf Steiner's death in 1925, a second esoteric school came into existence under the auspices of the Anthroposophical Society, newly re-founded in 1923/1924.

deck (at that time it was simply a deck of playing cards) was in fact the lost Book of Hermes, the great teacher of the Egyptians. It was this indication by Court de Gébelin that sparked interest in the Tarot as more than a deck of playing cards. It gradually became clear that the Tarot represents a path of spiritual schooling carried over in metamorphosed form from ancient Egypt, as will be shown in detail later.

This new wave of interest in the Tarot began in France toward the end of the eighteenth century. Since that time a great deal of literature has been published on this theme, particularly in French. In this literature the Tarot is spoken of both as the Book of Thoth and as the Book of Hermes. Hermes, also called Hermes Trismegistus, was the great teacher of the Egyptians, rather as Moses was the teacher of the people of Israel. The wisdom of Hermes came to expression through the oldest writings known from Egypt, called the Pyramid Texts.[1] Hermes was also said to be a representative on earth of the being known to the Egyptians as Thoth—the Egyptian god of wisdom. According to Rudolf Steiner:

> The Egyptian Book of Thoth consisted of 78 cards, which contained the world secrets. This was well known in the initiation rituals of Egypt. The names of the playing cards come from that King, Knight, Keeper of the Tower, Commander in Chief are esoteric denotations.[2]

The Tree of Life Represented by the Christmas Tree

The words quoted above are taken from a lecture held on December 12, 1906. Five days later, on December 17, 1906, as Christmas approached, Steiner gave a lecture about the significance of the

---

1. The building of the pyramids goes back some two and a half millennia before the Christian era. We are talking about a very ancient impulse that came through Hermes to the people of Egypt.

2. Rudolf Steiner, *The Misraim Service* (Gt. Barrington, MA: Steiner Books, 2006), p. 375.

Christmas tree. Now this may seem rather far away from our theme, but it actually has very much to do with it. For although in our time we take the Christmas tree for granted, when we trace the origin of the Christmas tree back to about the sixteenth century we find that at that time the Christmas tree was felt to represent the Tree of Life, the tree belonging to paradise in the biblical account. The Christmas tree was intended originally to remind us of the Tree of Life from paradise.

When it was introduced, no one could have imagined that one day it would stand in shopping malls all around the world, denuded of what it was originally intended to represent, namely the Tree of Life, the tree that was barred from access to humanity at the time of the great event known as the Fall.

In early Christianity, however, it was known in some esoteric circles that with the coming of Christ the Tree of Life had come down upon the earth. This was a great and profound mystery. Up until the present time very few people have been able to penetrate this mystery.

The Christmas tree was intended to bring this esoteric mystery to expression. Rudolf Steiner attached great significance to the Christmas tree and indicated that the it should be appropriately decorated. When he held this Christmas lecture on December 17, 1906, he was standing next to a Christmas tree decorated according to his specific directions.

Certain symbols hung from the tree. We will go into the significance of these symbols, for this is relevant to our theme. And the Christmas tree was also decorated with thirty-three red wax candles, standing for the thirty-three years of the life of Christ. In front of each candle was a red rose made of wax. When the candle burned down it illuminated the rose. One can imagine this very beautiful sight of the Christmas tree with its thirty-three roses and thirty-three candles burning—and also the symbols hanging from the Christmas tree as indicated in the Figure 1.

In Figure 1 we see seven symbols arranged in the form of a cross. The image at the center of the cross formation is the symbol for the Tarot, comprising the Greek letters *Tau* and *Rho* together in a symbolic form.

The Tarot Symbol According to Rudolf Steiner

Let us first consider the significance of the Greek letters *Tau* and *Rho*. *Rho* has a very profound meaning. Observe how the letters are drawn. In our modern alphabet the letters are relatively abstract shapes. When we go back to the Greek or earlier alphabets, however, the shape of the letters still had a symbolic, imaginative, spiritual significance—as in the Hebrew language, for example.

Our letter "R" is derived from the Greek letter *Rho* (ρ), which is essentially a circle with a tail on it. Looking at the letter *Rho*, one can see that it is an imaginative representation of the human head and spinal column together. Thus *Rho* represents the human being. This is especially clear from the original Greek way of writing the letter *Rho* (as contrasted with the abstract typescript image of modern times).

On the other hand the *Tau* symbol relates to the very ancient impulse underlying the religion of Taoism.[1] Our letter "T" is

Figure 1

derived from the Greek letter *Tau* (τ). In the ancient Chinese religion Tao represented the force of nature, the force related to Isis in the ancient Egyptian mysteries. *Tau* represents the intelligent force of nature that is leading all the time to higher and higher levels of evolution. It is a force with which we

---

1. The letters "D" and "T" are phonetically equivalent. For example, God (English) is *Gott* in German. In this sense the words Daoism and Taoism are phonetically equivalent, as are the words Dao and Tao.

can connect and which guides humanity to ever higher levels on the evolutionary path.

The Tarot symbol made up of *Tau* and *Rho* represents a coming together of the force of nature, the inner spirit of nature (Tao), symbolized by the letter *Tau*, with that which is represented by the letter *Rho*, which has to do with the human soul. Tarot—*Tau* plus *Rho*—is very often translated as "the Way." It represents the way of the human soul incarnated in a physical body connected with the whole of nature (by virtue of being in a physical body here on the earth).

This is one level of understanding the Tarot symbol, and this was known in the ancient Egyptian mysteries. Here is what Rudolf Steiner says regarding this image in his lecture on the Christmas tree:

> Those who were initiated in the Egyptian mysteries were able to read ⳨ (the symbol for Tarot). They could also read the Book of Thoth, which comprised 78 cards in which all world events were depicted from the beginning to the end, from Alpha to Omega.[1]

Alpha and Omega: The Beginning and the End

If we look at the horizontal line of the cross in Figure 1, to the left of the Tarot symbol is "Alpha" (A) corresponding to our modern letter "A." To the right is "Omega" (Ω), from which our letter "O" is derived. Alpha and Omega are the first and last letters of the Greek alphabet. In this connection we may recall the expression used by Christ in the first chapter of Revelation when he appears to John. He says "I am the Alpha and the Omega . . . the first and the last. . . ." (Rev. 1:8,17). The beginning of evolution (Alpha = first) and the end of evolution (Omega = last): this is the horizontal stream of time indicated in the words of Rudolf Steiner:

1. Rudolf Steiner, *The Misraim Service* (Great Barrington, MA: Steiner Books, 2006), p. 375.

They could also read the Book of Thoth, which comprised 78 cards in which all world events were depicted from the beginning to the end, from Alpha to Omega, and which one could decipher if they were arranged in their proper order. The book contained pictures of life, leading to death and arising again to new life. Whoever could combine the correct numbers with the correct pictures could read what was written. And this number knowledge, this picture knowledge, had been taught from earliest times. It also still had a great influence in the Middle Ages, as for instance on Raymond Lully (twelfth / thirteenth centuries), but nowadays not much of it remains.[1]

Steiner indicates with these words that the Tarot has a great deal to do with mystery wisdom and that it has to do with reading the Egyptian Book of Thoth, the Book of Hermes.

The Significance of the Symbols on the Christmas Tree

Let us now consider the connection of the symbols in Figure 1 with the vertical axis. The square at the bottom represents the fourfold human being. The human being comprising a physical body, a life body, a soul body, and a spirit (the conscious "I")—that is what the fourfold figure, the square, represents.

Above it is the triangle that represents the spiritual members of the human being, which are in a process of development and will come to full expression only in the far-distant future. These spiritual members are referred to in the Hindu tradition as Manas, Buddhi, and Atma. Rudolf Steiner uses the expression Spirit Self for Manas, Life Spirit for Buddhi, and Spirit Human for Atma.

The square and the triangle together represent the sevenfold nature of the human being in the process of evolutionary development. Continuing this ascent, above the square and the triangle, we come to the Tarot symbol. The Tarot represents something that has to do with the human being, but also goes beyond, for the

---

1. Op. cit., pp. 375–376.

Tarot "depicts all world events from beginning to end." Then, continuing to ascend the vertical axis in Figure 1, we rise beyond the Tarot symbol. We recognize that the symbol above that of the Tarot is the Ankh symbol from ancient Egypt, which is connected with what Christ refers to as the Bread of Life. (Christ refers to himself as the Bread of Life.) The Ankh symbol comprises the Greek letter *Tau* with a circle above it. As referred to above, the *Tau* is a symbol for the spiritual in nature, what is also known as the Earth Mother, whom the Greeks called Demeter and whom the Egyptians referred to as Isis. And the circle is a symbol for the Heavenly Father represented by Osiris. These two come together in the Ankh symbol.

Above the Ankh symbol we see the symbol of the five-pointed star, which represents the human being of the future, at the end of the cycle of evolution. The star crowning the Christmas tree symbolizes the goal we are evolving toward.

The symbols along the vertical axis of Figure 1 indicate to us a path of ascent in the vertical, and the symbols belonging to the horizontal axis show us the stream of time.

Most significant is that the Tarot symbol lies in the middle of the cross in Figure 1. The Tarot is at the heart of this cross. If we can penetrate the meaning of the Tarot symbol, we are able to arrive at the heart of the matter.

Cosmic Stages of Evolution

We shall now consider the symbols arranged in such a way that a completely new set of symbols is added to the original cross formation—see Figure 2.

In Figure 2 we see that something has been added to the cross arrangement in Figure 1. Let us recall that with Figure 1 we looked at the symbols on the Christmas tree together with the thirty-three red candles and the thirty-three red roses. These symbols were arranged in the form depicted in Figure 1, that of a cross, according to Rudolf Steiner's indications in the year 1906.

In the year 1911, five years later, on the Christmas tree that Rudolf Steiner had decorated at that time, we see from Figure 2 the addition of the planetary symbols forming an "S" curve around the structure of the cross, and also that the Tarot symbol is somewhat lower (relative to its position in Figure 1). These details are all very significant.

Now we need to understand the planetary symbols, which are arranged in the form of a letter "S" around the vertical axis of the

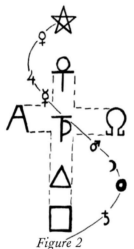

Figure 2

cross. This reminds us of the symbol used in medicine, the Staff of Mercury, the staff with the "S" form around it (usually with two "S" curves around the vertical axis— one of them a mirror image of the other).

The sequence of planets begins at the bottom with the symbol for the planet Saturn. Then comes the symbol for the Sun, followed by the symbol for the Moon as we ascend the "S" curve. From these three symbols we recognize that they follow the sequence of the planets as they are named in the cycle of the days of the week. Saturday is named after Saturn;

Sunday after the Sun; Monday after the Moon.

Continuing further up the "S" curve, we discover that the subsequent planetary symbols continue in the sequence corresponding to the names of the days of the week. Thus, Tuesday (Mardi in French) corresponds to Mars, Wednesday (Mercredi in French) is the day of Mercury, Thursday (Jeudi in French) corresponds to Jupiter, and Friday (Vendredi in French) is the day sacred to Venus. This is precisely the sequence of the planetary symbols ascending the "S" curve in Figure 2, as may be seen from Table One.

Hermeticism Lecture 2008

Table One

Days of Week	Days in French	Planetary Correspondence
Saturday	Samedi	Saturn
Sunday	Dimanche	Sun
Monday	Lundi	Moon
Tuesday	Mardi	Mars
Wednesday	Mercredi	Mercury
Thursday	Jeudi	Jupiter
Friday	Vendredi	Venus

Since the names of the planets are Latin, the names for the days of the week in a Latin-based language such as French can be seen to correspond more closely with these names than in a language like English. The ascending S-curve of planets—Saturn, Sun, Moon, Mars, Mercury, Jupiter, Venus—culminates with the symbol of the five-pointed star, which shows the goal, the final stage of evolution. The ascending sequence of planetary symbols, culminate with the five-pointed star, which crowns the vertical axis of symbols leading up from the square and the triangle.

In Figure 2, why is the Tarot symbol lower in comparison with its position in Figure 1? Evidently this was very important to Rudolf Steiner. The crossing point of the "T" of the Tau symbol is in the exact middle between the Alpha and the Omega, and it is also in the exact middle of the line connecting Mars and Mercury. This is because the Tarot symbol is moved down in Figure 2. In order to understand the deeper reason for this, we need to fill in some background.

One of Rudolf Steiner's greatest contributions to humanity is his depiction of the stages of cosmic evolution. He describes the evolutionary stages of our solar system, pointing out that before our present earth was formed there were three preceding cosmic stages of evolution. These were called Ancient Saturn, Ancient Sun, and Ancient Moon. According to Rudolf Steiner's description we are now—with the present earth—at the fourth stage of evolution. He describes how the fourfold nature of the human being has come into existence through these four stages of cosmic evolution.

He presents a profound cosmology that we cannot to go into here in much detail, other than to provide an overview. After these three preceding stages comes the earth stage of evolution, which is divided into two halves. The first half is the incarnating or descending phase, which has to do with the planet Mars. The second half, which is the current ascending phase of earthly evolution, has to do with the planet Mercury.

At the middle of the earth evolution there took place the event of the incarnation of Christ. This event signified the coming of the Tree of Life to the earth—the giving or bestowal of new life by Christ—so that the earth and humanity could begin to ascend to spiritual realms, following the path of ascent from Mercury to Jupiter, then to Venus, and then to the final stage of evolution.

Albrecht Altdorfer: "The Crucifixion"

A very profound symbolism comes to expression in many depictions of the crucifixion. This symbolism can be seen in a remarkable way in a painting by the German painter Albrecht Altdorfer entitled "The Crucifixion" from the year 1526 (image on page 53).

Looking at this image of the crucified Christ painted by Altdorfer, the cross is in the form of a *Tau* and the position of Christ hanging on the cross reminds us of a *Rho*. We see that the figure of Christ crucified bears a resemblance to the image of the Tarot symbol.

It was perhaps this deeper connotation to which Rudolf Steiner was drawing attention in his use of the symbols on the Christmas tree—that is, to the event of the crucifixion as the moment of the in-pouring of the Divine Spirit, the coming of the Tree of Life, the bestowal of the life blood for the regeneration of the earth and

humankind. In other words, Rudolf Steiner was indicating the beginning of a new phase of evolution, what is called in esoteric language the "Mercury" phase, an ascending phase of evolution, that began with the event known as the Mystery of Golgotha, comprising the crucifixion and the resurrection. For this is what emerges when we contemplate the crucifixion in relation to the Tarot symbol in the midst of the symbols on the Christmas tree.

In discovering that the figure of Christ crucified bears a resemblance to the image of the Tarot symbol, we find evidence of a remarkable presentiment that lived in the ancient Egyptian mysteries. This is one of the most extraordinary things revealed through a study of the Egyptian mysteries—that everything in the Egyptian mysteries having to do with Osiris prefigures what took place later in the life of Christ. The Osiris mythology relates precisely to the mystery of death and resurrection lived through by Christ.

Mark, Ormus, and the Misraim Service

Let us consider, for example, the experience of Mark, the author of the Gospel of St. Mark. After accompanying the Apostle Peter to Rome, he then went to Alexandria and worked there together with an Egyptian priest, Ormus, who was an initiate in the Egyptian mysteries. Together they developed the Misraim service, which was a Christianized version of one of the ancient Egyptian mystery rituals. As a point of reference for deepening into this meeting of Christianity with the Egyptian mysteries, I can recommend the book *The Misraim Service* by Rudolf Steiner, which is also known under the title *Freemasonry and Ritual Work*. This book is in the stream of Freemasonry that connects onto the work of Mark. "Misraim" is the Hebrew name for Egypt, and refers also to the legendary first Pharaoh Menes (Hebrew: Misraim) from whom the land of Egypt derived its name. When Mark went to Egypt, he experienced an extraordinary openness to his message concerning Jesus of Nazareth, the Messiah, who had been crucified and on the third day had risen from the dead.

The Egyptians accepted this message more or less as a matter of course because they were familiar with the mythology of the death and resurrection of Osiris. They understood immediately that Christ Jesus was like Osiris, who underwent death and resurrection. Seen in this light, the Egyptian mysteries were a preparation for the great event lived out on the historical plane by Christ—even down to the detail that the Tarot symbol portrayed the mystery of the Son of Man nailed to the world cross, as the Tree of Life bringing new life to all humanity.

This was prefigured in the Egyptian mysteries, and it was to this that Rudolf Steiner was drawing attention in holding his lectures on the mystery of the Christmas tree, presenting the Tarot at the center of the structure of the arrangement of the symbols on the Christmas tree.

The Seven Levels of the Human Being and the Lord's Prayer

Earlier I mentioned the complementary nature of two spiritual paths. There is on the one hand what Rudolf Steiner was drawing attention to above, and on the other there is what is presented as a spiritual path in the book *Meditations on the Tarot*. This however is a big theme concerning which we can only give a brief outline.

Let us first consider the symbol of the *square* and the *triangle* beneath the Tarot symbol on the Christmas tree. The square relates to the mystery of the fourfold human being and the triangle to the three spiritual members over and above the fourfold human being. The mystery of the seven levels of the human being is addressed in the central prayer that Christ taught, known as the "Our Father" or Lord's prayer. This prayer has seven petitions, each relating to a level in the human being. For example, the petition "Give us this day our daily bread" relates to the *physical* body, which is evident when we consider that it is the daily bread that maintains the physical body.

"Forgive us our trespasses as we forgive those who trespass against us" is the petition that relates to the level of the life body, also known as the *etheric* body. Simply by virtue of living here on the earth we cannot help but now and again trespass against other people—for example, if somebody says: "You are blocking my view." We have to learn to forgive. The teaching of Christ is: "Forgive us our trespasses as we forgive those who trespass against us." In other words, to the extent that we forgive others, we can also be forgiven for what we do.

Then there is the petition "Lead us not into temptation," which is directed to the human soul body, also known as the *astral* body. It is the soul level of the human being that is tempted. There are various kinds of temptations. This petition is not to be understood as a prayer to God literally not to lead us into temptation. Rather, it is a turning to God to request the strength and the power to withstand temptation. A more correct formulation would be, "Let us not enter into temptation." In other words, the request is for the bestowal of spiritual strength sufficient to enable us to withstand the lure of temptation.

Then we come to the petition, "Deliver us from evil." This petition is related to the level of the *Ego* (the conscious "I") in the human being, which has to choose between good and evil.

The symbol of the square relates to these four petitions of the Lord's prayer, as just described in relation to the fourfold human being comprising a physical body, etheric (life) body, astral (soul) body, and Ego or conscious "I."

Now let us consider the symbol of the triangle in relation to the first three petitions of the "Our Father" prayer. Preceding the first three petitions are the words, "Our Father who art in heaven," known as the "address to the Father" at the beginning of the prayer. Then follow the three petitions: "Hallowed be thy name," "Thy kingdom come," and "Thy will be done." These three petitions relate to the three higher members of the human being comprising the triangle. This is the level of *Manas*, *Buddhi*, and *Atma*—also known as Spirit Self, Life Spirit, and Spirit Human, the latter signifying the resurrected human being of the distant future, the ultimate goal of human evolution.

Table of Correspondences

	Seven Levels		*Petitions of the Lord's Prayer*
7	Atma—Spirit Human	3	Thy will be done
6	Buddhi—Life Spirit	2	They kingdom come
5	Manas—Spirit Self	1	Hallowed be thy name
4	Ego or "I"	7	Deliver us from evil
3	Astral (Soul) Body	6	Lead us not into temptation
2	Etheric (Life) Body	5	Forgive us our trespasses
1	Physical Body	4	Give us this day our daily bread

The symbols of the square and the triangle taken together underlie this teaching of the esoteric meaning of the Lord's prayer. Before writing *Meditations on the Tarot*, its anonymous author entered into the spiritual significance of the "Our Father" prayer in a very profound way. We see that his spiritual striving relates to the vertical axis of the structure of the Christmas tree symbols. This is the path he followed. It is the path from an understanding of the esoteric dimension of the Lord's prayer, symbolized by the square and the triangle, to the next symbol, that of the Tarot. Moreover, in his work dedicated to an understanding of the raising of Lazarus from the dead (see below) he was evidently also striving to reach up still higher on this vertical axis, to that which is represented by the Ankh symbol. This was the greatest miracle performed by Christ. It was this miracle that led the Scribes and Pharisees to decide that he should be crucified, as described in chapter 12 of the Gospel of St. John.

The Ankh Symbol on the Christmas Tree

The Ankh symbol relates to the Bread of Life. It was Christ Jesus who said of himself, "I am the bread of life." This mystery of the Bread of Life was entrusted by Christ to Lazarus, whom he raised from the dead. After writing *Meditations on the Tarot*, the author's next—and last—work was entitled *Lazarus, Come Forth!* (the first English edition was entitled *Covenant of the Heart*). In this final work the author tries to come to an understanding of the raising of Lazarus from the dead, the greatest of all of Christ's miracles. And this miracle encapsulates the mystery of the Bread of Life, to which the Ankh symbol refers. What I am saying here about this mystery is expressed in a greatly abbreviated way, for it would take too long now to try to unravel it in detail. In essence, it is a matter of trying to give a picture of the spiritual path followed by the author of *Meditations on the Tarot*, the path represented in the vertical axis of the structure of the symbols of the Christmas tree.

On the other hand, the spiritual path followed by Rudolf Steiner is outlined in the "S" curve winding around the vertical axis of the structure of the Christmas tree symbols. The "S" curve relates to the stages of planetary evolution, and Rudolf Steiner is the one who gave humanity such a profound teaching concerning the cosmic stages of evolution.

The Interweaving of Two Spiritual Paths

If we bring these two paths together—the path depicted by the vertical axis and the path outlined by the "S" curve winding around the vertical axis—we have the symbol known as the Staff  of Mercury, which is a symbol of the healing impulse. Taking these two together leads to an extraordinary fructification. In broad terms, this fructification is an expression of the of the interweaving of these two great teachers of the twentieth century, who followed the two spiritual paths outlined here.[1] For both of them—as both were Christ initiates of the twentieth century—the central focus of their work was to present the Christ mystery to humanity. As is revealed through contemplating the structure of the symbols of the Christmas tree with the Tarot symbol at the center, this is the symbol *par excellence* for representing the Christ mystery.

The Christ mystery, focused upon the Mystery of Golgotha, is the most profound aspect of what is revealed by Rudolf Steiner in his life's work. We do not know how he actually worked with the Tarot cards in the first esoteric school. However we do know that he attached great significance to the Tarot, placing it at the center of the symbols he positioned so precisely on the Christmas tree. From this we begin to see something of the extraordinary significance and magnitude of what lives in the Tarot.

Rudolf Steiner could not do everything, however. He knew that other spiritual teachers would come after him, and that there would be one who would penetrate the deeper mysteries of the Lord's prayer and of the Tarot. From an understanding of the symbols as

---

1. It is an over-simplification to express the spiritual paths of these two teachers solely in terms of the vertical axis and the "S" curve winding around the vertical axis, since both teachers participate to a certain degree in the entire form of the Staff of Mercury that their interweaving represents.

positioned along the vertical axis of the Christmas tree, it is evident that still higher mysteries remain—those connected with the Ankh symbol and with the five-pointed star. And there are yet other spiritual teachers whose task it is to unravel these mysteries.

To summarize, we need to grasp the central significance of the Tarot—the lost Book of Hermes or Book of Thoth—as something of great spiritual value, which we are now able with the help of *Meditations on the Tarot* to read in a new way.

The Horizontal Axis and the Divine Personality

Let us now consider the horizontal axis of the structure of the symbols on the Christmas tree. The horizontal axis relates to the flow of time from the beginning (Alpha) to the end (Omega). Now it is the divine personality represented on the cross who said of himself "I am the Alpha and the Omega," as we read in the first chapter of Revelation. This divine human personality appeared to John as a cosmic manifestation and spoke the words recorded in Revelation, indicating that he is a cosmic being. In Jewish tradition he is referred to as the Messiah. In Revelation he is called the Lamb of God. In the Persian tradition he is known as Soshyans, the Saviour (literally, "he who brings benefit").

He is the one whom many of the ancient religions were awaiting, the one whom many peoples of antiquity were expecting. He is the one who came to bring about the great transition in humankind's evolution on the earth. As was understood in early Christianity, he brought the Tree of Life down to earth. Thus the diagram showing the structure of the symbols of the Christmas tree (Figure 2) is understandable only if one also includes (represented by the horizontal axis) this cosmic being who said of himself, "I am the Alpha and the Omega."

Symbolically one could say, in terms of the cross, that the horizontal axis represents the stream of time and the vertical axis represents space between the above and the below. The quintessential teaching in *Meditations on the Tarot* was taught already some 4,500 years ago by Hermes: "As above, so below." In other words, there is a correspondence between the heavens and the earth. What is added in *Meditations on the Tarot* is the application of this symbolism to the stream of time, as indicated by the words: "What was, will be." In other words, what has taken place in the past reappears at a later time in a metamorphosed form.

Osiris—Isis—Nephthys—Horus

Continuing the theme of the Tarot as a resurrection of the Egyptian mysteries, let us now consider the way in which the twenty-two Major Arcana of the Tarot are presented in *Meditations on the Tarot*. Clearly, the first four Major Arcana are of great significance, for they outline the spiritual path of Christian Hermeticism. Contemplating the first four Major Arcana, the author draws a relationship with the four letters of the name of God in the Hebrew tradition: YOD-HÉ-VAU-HÉ. This is the Tetragrammaton of the Hebrew mysteries. It was so sacred that it was generally not spoken, being considered the unutterable name of God. These four letters refer to four different levels of spiritual reality.

These four levels were known in the Egyptian mysteries. There they were related directly to divine beings. Let us contemplate the image of the first Major Arcanum, that of the Magician. What underlies this image? It is the great initiation.

For the Egyptians, though they had a multitude of gods, the main focus of their religion was Osiris. What stands behind the image of the Magician depicted in the first Arcanum? In the sense of the Egyptian mysteries this image could be called the Arcanum of Osiris.

One of the most extraordinary revelations brought by Rudolf Steiner was his identification of Osiris, whom he indicated to be the Christ in his pre-incarnatory form. When Hermes, who was regarded as the founder of the Egyptian mysteries, spoke of Osiris and Isis, he spoke as an initiate who was able to behold Christ in his pre-incarnatory form, whom he called Osiris. This identification is the key to a profound level of understanding. Similarly, Hermes was also able to behold Sophia in her pre-incarnatory form, and he called her Isis.

Hermes is said to have introduced the worship of Osiris and Isis into the Egyptian mysteries, and when he spoke of Osiris and Isis he was referring to Christ and Sophia in their pre-incarnatory forms. Now we say Christ and Sophia. The Egyptians spoke of Osiris and Isis. In the language of Revelation they are referred to as the Lamb and his Bride. Thus the first Arcanum of the Tarot is the Arcanum of the Lamb/Christ/Osiris, and it is about the meeting with this being in the great initiation.

Just as the first Major Arcanum of the Tarot is the Arcanum of Osiris, so is the second Arcanum that of Isis, understood in the sense of the ancient Egyptians. One can follow this in every detail if one enters into the mystery language spoken in the Egyptian mysteries leading to this great all-embracing mystery of Osiris and Isis.

In terms of the images represented on the cards of the Major Arcana of the Tarot, the image of the *first* Arcanum is that of the Magician and that of the *second* Arcanum is the High Priestess. The Magician symbolizes Osiris and the High Priestess symbolizes the great goddess Isis.

The image presented on the card of the *third* Arcanum is that of the Empress. In terms of the Egyptian mysteries the image of the third Arcanum is a symbolic representation of the goddess Nephthys, who is the sister of Isis. In the mysteries relating to the death and resurrection of Osiris both Isis and Nephthys play a role. Isis is depicted holding the barque, or boat, of the Sun, in which Osiris ascends to the heavens, emerging from the underworld at sunrise. Nephthys is shown accompanying Osiris on his path of descent into the underworld at the time of sunset. The two sisters stand at the head and feet of Osiris, the Sun Spirit, the head being associated with sunrise (Isis) and the feet with sunset (Nephthys).

When we look at the *fourth* card of the Major Arcana of the Tarot, we find the image of the Emperor, corresponding to the pharaoh in the Egyptian mysteries. The pharaoh stood under the direct protection of Horus, the son of Isis and Osiris. The fourth card thus represents Horus, who is the protector of the pharaoh. The Emperor is under the sign of Horus, just as the Magician, the High Priestess, and the Empress relate to Osiris, Isis, and Nephthys. In the first four cards of the Major Arcana of the Tarot we thus find a resurrection of the mysteries of ancient Egypt connected with Osiris, Isis, Nephthys, and Horus.

In the Egyptian mysteries Nephthys was associated particularly with *magical* powers, and the third Arcanum of the Tarot, relating to the Empress, is described in *Meditations on the Tarot* as the Arcanum of *sacred magic*, which is the result of the alignment of human will with divine will. Similarly, for the ancient Egyptians Isis is the goddess who signifies the personification of cosmic *wisdom*, and the second Arcanum, represented by the image of the High Priestess, is described in *Meditations on the Tarot* as the Arcanum of *gnosis* or *divine knowing*—the faculty through which one attains cosmic wisdom.

In the religion of ancient Egypt Osiris represented the goal. *Union* with Osiris was the aspiration of participants in the Egyptian mysteries. Likewise, the goal outlined in the first Major Arcanum of the Tarot, represented by the image of the Magician, is the *mystical union* with the cosmic being of Christ through the great initiation. Christ went through death and resurrection and has thereby become the guide of human beings towards our ultimate goal of evolution, which is the resurrection.

Regarding the association of Horus with the fourth Arcanum, the Emperor, see the discussion on the next two pages.

Obviously there are many other connections to be made between the images of the Tarot and the Egyptian mysteries. For example, if one looks at the card of the eighth Arcanum, one sees a female figure holding the scales of justice. This is clearly related to the goddess Maat, who holds the scales in the Egyptian mysteries, weighing the souls of the deceased in the judgment hall of Osiris in the life after death.

Hermeticism Lecture 2008

Correspondences Between the Divine and Human Levels

As indicated briefly already, everything that was prepared in the ancient mysteries was realized in the life of Christ Jesus as the embodiment of Osiris. Moreover, against this background the Virgin Mary can be seen as an earthly representative of Isis, and Mary Magdalene as an earthly representative of Nephthys. The two women were at the foot of the cross during the crucifixion and were also present at the laying in the grave—Mary at the head and Mary Magdalene at the feet of Christ Jesus, just as Isis and Nephthys are depicted at the head and the feet of Osiris.

Moreover, the Apostle John, with whom Lazarus was spiritually united,[1] was also present at the foot of the cross and at the laying in the grave. If we consider the fourth Arcanum, the Emperor, in relation to Horus, something very interesting emerges when we contemplate the raising of Lazarus from the dead. This was an initiation performed by Christ on Lazarus—a great initiation in which Lazarus was raised from the dead. This initiation reminds us of the initiation of the Egyptian pharaohs that took place in the King's Chamber of the Great Pyramid. The sarcophagus was not there for the purpose of the burial rite of the pharaoh, but rather for his initiation rite. The pharaoh lay in the sarcophagus and "died" into Osiris, entering a death-like state that lasted for about three days, and then returned to earthly existence having received new life from Osiris, enabling him to rule the people as an initiate-king, as a "son" of Osiris.

Similarly, Lazarus died and was placed into a sarcophagus in the family tomb near his home in Bethany, having died into Christ through his close inner relationship with Jesus. Christ, having been summoned to Bethany by Lazarus' sisters Martha and Mary Magdalene, went down into the tomb and called the soul of the

---

1. Robert Powell, *The Mystery, Biography & Destiny of Mary Magdalene: Sister of Lazarus-John & Spiritual Sister of Jesus* (Great Barrington, MA: Steiner Books, 2008), chapter 3, "The John Mystery."

deceased Lazarus back into his body, bestowing on him new life for the fulfillment of a great mission upon the earth. The raising of Lazarus from the dead through Christ was a re-enactment on earth of the initiation of the pharaohs in the Egyptian mysteries, who "died" into Osiris. Lazarus became the initiated one—in a spiritual sense the Emperor/Pharaoh, in light of this deeper understanding of the significance of the fourth Arcanum of the Tarot against the background of the Egyptian mysteries.

As described in my book *The Mystery, Biography & Destiny of Mary Magdalene*, Lazarus was the brother of Mary Magdalene. From an early age he was deeply connected with the Virgin Mary, and he was the spiritual brother of Jesus, the one whom Jesus loved, as is said in the eleventh chapter of the Gospel of St. John. Lazarus later took on the name of John and under that name wrote the Gospel of St. John as well as the Letters of John and Revelation. From the standpoint of the Egyptian mysteries, he is in the role of Horus as the spiritual son of Christ/Osiris through his initiation, having been raised from the dead. And just as Horus, the son of Osiris, continued the spiritual mission of his father, so Lazarus-John, since his initiation, has continued the work of Christ.

To summarize, a correspondence is evident from the divine to the human level, expressed in relation to the first four Major Arcana of the Tarot in the following table:

	Arcanum	Egyptian Mysteries	Christian Mysteries (divine level)	Christian Mysteries (human level)
I	Magician	Osiris	Christ	Jesus
II	High Priestess	Isis	Sophia	Mary
III	Empress	Nephthys	Holy Soul	Mary Magdalene
IV	Emperor	Horus	Holy Spirit	Lazarus-John

In the Christian mysteries a sixfoldness emerges when the Divine Masculine and Divine Feminine Trinities are juxtaposed, as described in the nineteenth Arcanum of *Meditations on the Tarot*, as indicated in the table below.

Divine Masculine	*Divine Feminine*
Father	Mother
Son (Christ)	Daughter (Sophia)
Holy Spirit	Holy Soul

Lazarus-John, having been initiated by Christ and continuing the work of Christ on earth, can be viewed as a representative on earth of the Holy Spirit, fulfilling the words of Christ: "I will send him [the Counselor, i.e. the Holy Spirit] to you. . . .When the Spirit of Truth comes, he will guide you into all the truth . . . and he will declare to you the things that are to come" (John 16:7, 13). What is Revelation if not a revelation of "the things that are to come"? And on this account it is called the Testament of the Holy Spirit, just as the Old Testament is the Testament of the Father, and the New Testament is the Testament of the Son. Lazarus-John is clearly indicated as one through whom the Counselor, the Holy Spirit, has spoken—and, in the sense of his eternal individuality, speaks now and will continue to speak in the future.

Similarly, Mary Magdalene, who was also initiated by Christ,[1] can be viewed as a representative on earth of the Holy Soul, the feminine counterpart of the Holy Spirit. The brother-sister relationship of these two Christ initiates—Lazarus-John and Mary Magdalene—mirrors on earth the divine level of the relationship between the Holy Spirit and the Holy Soul.

---

1. Robert Powell, op. cit., pp. 10–11.

Meditations on the Tarot and the Catholic Church

It is well known that there are many new ideas coming from the Catholic Church and that Catholic theologians are writing new and profound things. For example there is a book entitled *The Maternal Face of God*, by Leonardo Boff (1987), in which the thesis is put forward that the Virgin Mary was an incarnation of the Holy Spirit and that she was—as a perfect human being—a forerunner of humanity of the future.

It is quite evident that, through *Meditations on the Tarot* and other works, esoteric Christianity is being introduced into the Catholic Church, stimulating many of the new ideas now surfacing among Catholic theologians. We need only recall that *Meditations on the Tarot* has been translated into Spanish, Portuguese, Italian, Russian, German, French, and English. There is even a photograph of Pope John Paul II with a copy of the hardbound two-volume German edition of *Meditations of the Tarot* on his desk.

The latest edition of *Meditations on the Tarot* has several wonderful endorsements printed on the back cover. One of them is by Bede Griffiths, who was one of the people who originally endorsed this book. Bede Griffiths is no longer alive. He was a Catholic priest who founded an Ashram in Southern India. He studied the Hindu tradition very deeply. When he came across *Meditations on the Tarot*, he became so passionately interested in it that his vision was to found a community with each person in the community representing one of the Tarot cards (excepting the fifteenth Arcanum, the Devil). He himself wanted to be the Hermit, as this was his favorite Tarot card.

Hans Urs von Balthasar was invited by Herder, a major German publisher, to write a Foreword to the German edition. I did not think it appropriate as a Foreword, and so in the English edition it appears as an Afterword. Hans Urs Von Balthasar is looked upon by many as the leading Catholic theologian of the twentieth century. His output of books is astonishing. In fact, it is difficult to believe he could have written so many. Generally they are extensive and erudite books on many different theological topics. Hans Urs von Balthasar was also the spiritual advisor of Adrienne von Speyr, a mystic who has written some wonderful books. Hans Urs von Balthasar was so respected that Pope John Paul II nominated him as a cardinal, but two days before he was due to receive the cardinal's vestments he died. The mission of the author of *Meditations on the Tarot* was to carry the stream of esoteric Christianity into the stream of exoteric Christianity represented by the Catholic Church, and thus it is of significance that the book received an endorsement from such an outstanding representative of the Roman Catholic Church as Cardinal Hans Urs von Balthasar.

The Divine Feminine

Another aspect of the mission of the author of *Meditations on the Tarot* becomes clear in connection with what he says regarding the "luminous Holy Trinity." He applies this expression to the three-fold aspect of the Divine Feminine: Mother, Daughter, and Holy Soul. The "luminous Holy Trinity" is in turn the key to the theology of the Divine Feminine, sometimes referred to as Sophiology—which, however, refers more specifically to the theology of Sophia, who corresponds to the Daughter in this Trinity. The "luminous Holy Trinity" is discussed in the nineteenth Arcanum of *Meditations on the Tarot*, and I have elaborated upon this in my books *The Sophia Teachings* and *The Most Holy Trinosophia*.

Some critics of the Christian-Hermetic approach to spirituality represented by *Meditations on the Tarot* maintain that the Divine Feminine is a kind of projection from the human level onto the divine level. While a plausible psychological case can be put forward for such a projection, this does not take into consideration the reference in Revelation to the Lamb and His Bride, meaning Christ and Sophia. It also does not consider the many testimonies to the Divine Feminine down through the ages, including the testimony of the German poet and playwright Goethe at the end of Part II of his great drama *Faust*:

Virgin, Mother, Queen,
Keep us, Goddess, in thy Grace!
All things corruptible
Are but a parable;
Earth's insufficiency
Here finds fulfillment;
Here the ineffable
Wins life through love;
The Eternal Feminine
Leads us above.

It can be problematic to endeavor to apply earthly terms to cosmic relationships. For example, when we use expressions such as God the Father or God the Son, we are at a different level than when speaking of father and son in ordinary language. In this connection what are we to make of the fact that the ancient Egyptians practiced marriage between brother and sister? This practice resulted, in part, from projecting divine cosmic relationships onto the earthly level. Osiris and Isis were seen as brother and sister and, simultaneously, as husband and wife—as in Revelation, which speaks of the Lamb and His Bride. This divine relationship means something very profound on a spiritual level and cannot simply be projected onto the earthly level as the ancient Egyptians did—in the belief that the pharaoh mirrored Osiris and as the pharaoh's wife mirrored Isis—the pharaoh's wife often being his sister, just as Isis was perceived to be simultaneously the wife and sister of Osiris. It is clear that this kind of projection from a spiritual to an earthly level is not to be conceived of in such a simple and literal way. What is clear, however, is that those drawn to the being of Sophia are particularly interested in the Isis mysteries and the resurrection of the Isis mysteries in a new form—recalling that Sophia was seen by the ancient Egyptians as Isis. And that is why the work of *Meditations on the Tarot* is central in this context, for it deals with the resurrection of the Egyptian mysteries.

Hermeticism Lecture 2008

Concluding Remarks

The stream of esoteric Christianity represented by the author of *Meditations on the Tarot* leads from the present Mercury stage of evolution to the future Jupiter stage, which is the next stage of evolution of the human being and the earth. Let us contemplate again the "S" curve of the diagram of the symbols of the Christmas tree (Figure 2). This "S" curve represents the stages of evolution in ascending order. The location of the Tarot symbol—at the center of the "S" curve and, at the same time, at the center of the horizontal and vertical axes of the cross—marks the place of the Mystery of Golgotha as the turning point of evolution from the descending Mars phase to the ascending Mercury. We saw, in relation to Albrecht Altdorfer's portrayal of the crucifixion how Christ on the cross bears a resemblance to the Tarot symbol. At the present time we are in the Mercury phase of evolution, some two thousand years on from the Mystery of Golgotha, the central turning point of time. Mercury leads to the next stage, future Jupiter. Recognition of the impulse leading from Mercury to Jupiter, as embodied in *Meditations on the Tarot*, illustrates the remarkable scope of the guidance of the spiritual teacher who wrote this book. For my part I would like to express how wonderful it is to meet together with fellow students who are part of this great school of Christian Hermeticism, a school that this great spiritual teacher has brought into existence as a modern path of Christian initiation, whose foundation can be traced to initiation into the ancient Egyptian mysteries of Osiris, Isis, Nephthys, and Horus: the first four Arcana of *Meditations on the Tarot*.

As a closing to our gathering today, as students of Christian Hermeticism let us remind ourselves of the spiritual practice indicated in the first Arcanum—concentration without effort—which underlies the entire sequence of the twenty-two Major Arcana of the Tarot. Here with the relevant passage from the first Arcanum:

> Concentration without effort—that is to say where there is nothing to suppress and where contemplation becomes as natural as breath-

ing and the beating of the heart—is the state of consciousness (i.e. thought, imagination, feeling, and will) of perfect calm, accompanied by the complete relaxation of the nerves and the muscles of the body. It is the profound silence of desires, of preoccupations, of the imagination, of the memory, and of discursive thought. One may say that the entire being becomes like the surface of calm water, reflecting the immense presence of the starry sky and its indescribable harmony. And the waters are deep, they are so deep! And the silence grows, ever increasing. What silence! Its growth takes place through regular waves which pass, one after the other, through your being: one wave of silence followed by another wave of profound silence, then again a wave of still more profound silence. . . .Have you ever drunk silence? If in the affirmative, you know what concentration without effort is. To begin with there are moments, subsequently minutes, then "quarters of an hour" for which complete silence or concentration without effort lasts. With time, the silence or concentration without effort becomes a fundamental element always present in the life of the soul.

PART TWO

The
Wandering Fool

or

Love and its Symbols

Early Studies on the Tarot

ARCANA XIV-XXII

XIV

Temperance

Aqua vitae
[Water of Life]

A. LAYOUT OF THE CARD

A woman *measures* out a drink.

As V (The Pope) is the guardian with respect to the dangers of the autonomous personality (☆), so XIV is the guardian (the guardian Angel) with respect to the dangers of *intoxication*, that is, to the danger that the personality drown in a drunken orgy of the "élan vital."

XIV mirrors V: the one signifies protection from the *inflated consciousness of self* that leads to *magic* (Faust); the other signifies protection from intoxication, from *losing* consciousness of self in the vital and psychic forces of the subconscious through *vitalistic mysticism*.

B. General Meaning

Sobriety versus *intoxication* or *intoxicating* practices = Temperance.

Vital intoxication (its forms: dionysian orgies, debauchery of the Khlystys,[1] the psychic drunkenness of the dervishes, mystical union with nature, etc.) is—or *can* be—a reaction to XIII (Death):

Faust quaffs the inebriating draught to end his life of servitude to *Death*: the subconscious life-forces can overwhelm sober consciousness as a reaction of the instinctive nature against the intellectual nature, of the life-forces against the head, where the principle of *Death* resides.

But Temperance is neither the Intellect (the Head) nor the subconscious (the instinctive drives)—it is a *winged woman*, that is to say the *supra-conscious*, which acts *in the manner of instinct*, yet is not instinct.

She is equable and tranquil enthusiasm, prone neither to ecstasy nor to despair. She is the continual flow of living and life-bestowing water from one vessel to the other—never exceeding due measure—which is joyous serenity or peaceful and light-filled adoration:

She pours not wine, but *living water*.

With Athena, Neith,[2] the Virgin of Israel, the Holy Virgin, there is

---

1. Khlysts or Khlysty was an underground sect in the late 17th, 18th, 19th, and early 20th century that split off the Russian Orthodox Church. "Khlyst," the name commonly applied to them, is a distortion of the name they used; the original name was the invented word "Khristovery," "Christ-believers"; their critics corrupted the name, mixing it with the word khlyst, meaning "a whip." The Khlysty renounced priesthood, holy books, and veneration of the saints. They believed in a possibility of direct communication with the Holy Spirit and of its embodiment in living people. The central idea of the Khlysty ideology was to practice asceticism. The Khlysty practiced the attainment of divine grace for sin in ecstatic rituals, *radeniya*, that were rumored to sometimes turn into sexual orgies. Flagellation was also rumored, possibly due to the similarity of their name to the word for "whip." Each cell was normally led by a male and a female leader, who were called the 'Christ' and the 'Mother of God' respectively. In 1910, Grigori Rasputin was accused of having been a Khlyst by Sofia Ivanovna Tyutcheva, a governess of the Grand Duchesses of Russia. [ED]

2. Neith, or Net, Egyptian goddess, patron deity of Saïs.

no intoxication—here there flows from the spring of living waters, constant and steady, the life fluid of culture—Athens, Florence, Weimar... the blossoming of *Classicism*, not *Romanticism*.

The *wings* of Temperance are not wings of ecstasy, but wings in the true esoteric sense: currents serving both spiritual hearing and spiritual touch.

The descending stages on the ladder of degradation are as follows:

wings (arms + wing-tips)
arms (separated from the wing-tips)
appendages
tentacles (organs solely for hoarding)

The six wings of the Seraphim are organs of action *and* of perception: above (one pair); horizontal (another pair); below (third pair). Winged 'locomotion', spiritual 'flight', is the choosing of the highest, subtlest currents—thus do we 'elevate' ourselves, etc.

But the *sursum corda*[3] by means of wings has nothing to do with intoxication; it is rather a serene, calm elevation of one's being—

The growth of the soul in grandeur.

Whence comes the fluid—or living water—poured from the blue vase into the red vase? From the *wings*—for they *draw* the 'waters from above the firmament'.

The two vases are the *measures* that hinder intoxication or surfeit of forces; one is the vase of *transmission*, the other of *reception*.

3. The *Sursum Corda* (Latin for 'Lift up your hearts') is the opening dialogue to the Preface of the Eucharistic Prayer in the liturgies of the Christian Church, dating back to the third century.

This is: 1. *nephesh* or *gouph*, or
            2. *ruach* and *nephesh*, or
            3. *neshamah* and *ruach*

(physical/material body, etheric/life body, astral/soul body)

The life-body 'pours' a refreshing and vivifying fluid into the material body; the soul body 'animates' the life-body; the spirit, the individuality, is the vase of transmission of divine grace—of the *yechidah*:

what is *within* the human being—that is the *blessing* coming from without. (The Pope, Card V—blessing the acolytes—is the Mediator for the others; Temperance *pours* from vase to vase—she is the interior *Mediatrix*.)

The source of the movement of the 'living water' thus lies *above*— and *wings* are needed to draw it forth.

Intoxication, as the opposing principle, is movement in the opposite direction—*from below upward*. It is the invasion of the nephesh by the electric forces of the gouph; of the ruach by the life-forces of the nephesh; of the neshamah by the soul forces of the ruach.

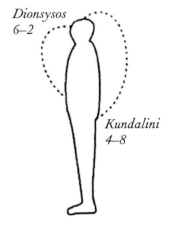

Dionsysos
6–2

Kundalini
4–8

Hatha Yoga training—whereby the Kundalini is caused to rise up into the head—is a folly, a training in madness; it is an intoxication of the most dangerous and disastrous kind possible, whereas a Dionysian intoxication is only temporary.

Temperance

C. *1. Mystical Meaning*

The water of life—mystical dew[4] (*life*) and mystical aridity.

2. Gnostic Meaning

The waters above the firmament and the waters below the firmament—(spiritual vitality and biological vitality—that is, the two kinds of *growing old*).

3. Magical Meaning

"The art of pouring from one vase into another"—

the art of restoring—repose, *vertical* respiration, 'to drink' interiorly—the art of *transforming* the spiritual into the soul, the soul into the vital, the vital into the physical.

Eliphas Lévi speaks of the werewolf, but it is a matter here of maintaining balance and health.

4. Philosophical Meaning

Transformism or evolution:

The mechanical does not 'evolve' into the organic, nor does the organic 'evolve' into the psychic, but the contrary: the psychic becomes vital, the vital becomes chemical and mechanical.

The lesser does not engender the greater, for it is only reduced from the maximum / optimum.

The *history* of humankind commences with the *fall* (minimalization); the history of the world commences with *Adam Kadmon*, who is the prototype, the efficient *and* final cause of evolution.

---

4. Dew = Dao / Tao (in German, *Tau*).

5. *Esoteric Meaning*

Meditative prayer or prayer-meditation fulfills the function of wings...
effecting the inner dew—the enlivening (*salvation*) of the soul, the
stimulation of vitality, and the restoration of the body's forces.

XV

The Devil

Non est bene hominem solum esse
[It is not good that the man should be alone]
Gen. 2:8

This card signifies the force of *intoxication*, as opposed to Temperance (as this latter is in turn opposed to Death).

It is the reflection of Card VI, *The Lovers*, which points to the choice between the life of temperance and that of intoxication.

A. LAYOUT OF THE CARD

A bisexual being with wing-tips stands on an altar, to which are chained two creatures of different sexes.

We immediately see: if VI poses the problem of *love*, XV poses that of *sex*.

We no longer have the winged spirit who inspires, but the wing-tipped devil who *directs*.

—Triangle: the bisexual (androgynous) devil and the two small devils of differing sex
—torch
—horns, the tails

B. General Meaning

The *devil*, and not Eliphas Lévi's neutral 'magical agent', for the figure on the altar is autonomous and dominating—nothing indicates that he acts on behalf of anyone else (the two below are agents, not of some magician, but of the devil).

Who is the devil?

1. He *exists*, for

(*a*) evil exists and cannot be attributed solely to God or to humanity;

(*b*) the Bible (Moses / Genesis, Job, Jesus Christ), and the Kabbalah attest the same;

(*c*) ignorance (*avidyā*) alone does not suffice to account for evil: *sin* exists, therefore *evil* exists; therefore the *author* of evil exists also.

2. Is the author of evil himself necessarily wicked? No. The analogy of human history teaches that much evil has been committed with a view to a good end ('the end justifies the means')—Emperor Constantine, the Inquisition, communism, etc.

The biblical (and kabbalistic) idea of the devil (Job, Samael—the prosecutor, the tempter, the 'strict letter of the law'—or the left side of the sephirothic tree, etc.)—*treaty*.

3. The fundamental facts of demonology—the three categories:

(*a*) the artificial creation of demons (Moloch, Sabbath goat, the Superman, etc.)—monstrous egregores.[1]

(*b*) the hierarchies of evil (eight, excepting the Seraphim)—the 'hierarchies of the Left'—who remain within the limits of the law (primal covenant or treaty)—their leader is the *Devil* (temptation and trials—never black magic).

---

1. "An egregore [is] an artificial being who owes his existence to collective generation *from below.*" *Meditations on the Tarot* (NY: Tarcher/Putnam, 2002, p139).

(c) human beings and other beings who have transgressed the Law (*black magic*, violent destruction, and depriving others of free will)—they do not have (and *cannot* have) a leader, because all 'fraternity' implies a sacrifice—which is precisely what they are incapable of. 'Fraternities' of black magicians therefore do not exist—not anywhere.

4. And the general meaning of Card XV?

False androgyny—the spirit of perversion and the intoxication of perversion. There are three ways to neutralize these binaries:[2]

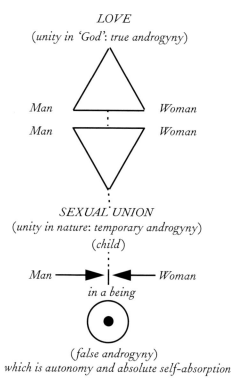

LOVE
(*unity in 'God': true androgyny*)

Man   Woman

Man   Woman

SEXUAL UNION
(*unity in nature: temporary androgyny*)
(*child*)

Man ———▶ ┆ ◀——— Woman
in a being

(*false androgyny*)
which is autonomy and absolute self-absorption

---

2. "Modern hermetic literature (of the nineteenth and twentieth centuries) takes account of the 'neutralization of binaries', that is, the method where one finds the *third*

Now, the devil of Card XV is bisexual: he suffices unto himself (= perversion). The smaller he-devil and she-devil below him are chained to his pedestal: *he* is their *ideal*, and the one does not seek the other in order to find the *other*, but to make the other a part of *itself*—they aspire to the ideal of androgyny; they do not desire each other except with a view to swallowing up or assimilating the other, driven (enchained) as they are by the desire to become androgynous.

Their tails, their *backbones*, are twice as long, signifying the *sub-natural* (their position being *vertical*—whereas with animals it is *horizontal*) nature of their will. The wing-tips of the devil signify the possibility of *autonomous* flight, not by means of 'wings', which enable one to be drawn up by spiritual currents from above, but flight 'in spite of' spiritual currents—*isolated* movement.

To which of these three categories does the devil of the card belong? Is he an egregore? A being of the hierarchies of evil? Or even a fallen being entirely outside the Law?

He is a creature (creation) of the egoistic desire for *freedom* (from gender)—called by from the marriage of *debauchery and asceticism*. He has become real—

And Here is the Lesson of the Card:

Whether you aspire to freedom beyond the attraction of man and woman (his right hand gesturing upward) or whether you follow the light and warmth of unrestrained desire (his left hand holding a burning torch) makes no difference; for in either case you *serve* him, for what you *really* desire is he, who encompasses both sexes, and who is free of the universal attraction, being attracted to one-self through oneself in oneself.

---

term, or neutral term, for the two terms ('binary') corresponding to the active and passive principles." *Meditations on the Tarot* (NY: Tarcher/Putnam, 2002, p 218).

C. *1. Mystical Meaning*

Adam-Hevah (Isch-Ischah)[3]

2. Gnostic Meaning

Syzygy and non-trinitarian 'Monotheism'.

3. Magical Meaning

The law of polarity; mechanical and sexual electricity, a *closed circuit* (in a single being)—procreation above, procreation below ✡; *sterility* (physical, soul, spiritual).

4. Philosophical Meaning

 antinomies—their *opposition, synthesis, mixture*, and *being compromise*.

5. Esoteric Meaning

The anti-resurrection body, which *does not die* and does not pass through death, being too 'solid' (closed circuit) for death—a *fortress*, because love and death are linked.
Infernal immortality opposing *celestial* immortality.

 True androgyny

---

3. Adam = first man; Hevah = Eve = first woman; Isch = Man; Ischah = Woman.

XVI

The Tower

Magnificat
[My soul doth] magnify [the Lord]
Luke 1:46

A. LAYOUT OF THE CARD

An 'edifice' or stronghold against destruction through death—built up in accordance with Card XV (the strength of false androgyny, or self-sufficiency, or the self-explanatory, contradiction-free *system*—an *absolute* system—whatsoever the philosophy or method)—*demands* and provokes an intervention from above: a *bolt of lightning*, that is to say an encounter with higher reality, which assumes the character of a 'collision', whereas an encounter with the same reality by an *'open'* organism yields the experience of 'blessing' and 'grace'.

Every *closed* system (Tower of Babel) is an expression of the desire for 'self-sufficiency' that is incarnated in the androgyny of the Devil of the XVth Arcanum.

82

The Tower

Paul Marteau (*The Tarot of Marseille*):

> "The Tower signifies that every edifice erected by human hands is destined for destruction, regardless whether that edifice be mental or physical, because everything that takes matter as its basis must disappear."[1]

The card's teaching: what is accomplished (the tower's crenellated crown) will be destroyed—one must not create *worlds* that are *autonomous* (independent) in the *world*, either mentally (systems) or morally (superhuman or perfected virtues) or in one's fantasy (illusions).

B. General Meaning

Psychological 'complexes', philosophical 'systems' (cancerous illnesses), closed social 'cliques', 'occult fraternities', 'idiots' (ἰδιῶται)[2]—are all subject to the law of the *Tower of Babel*: they can neither withstand nor survive the encounter with *Reality*.

(This pertains also to the arts: poetry, music, painting, etc.— *'eccentrics'*, innovators, so-called 'revolutionaries'—the Muses are *living beings* (organisms), and those who shut themselves off from their *life* condemn themselves to a 'fall'—*decadence*).

The law of *decadence*.

C. 1. Mystical Meaning

The Word of God ("all things were made through the Word, and nothing that was made was made without the Word").[3]

---

1. *Le Tarot de Marseille* (Paris: Arts et Metiers Graphiques, 1949).
2. The Greek term 'idiot' was originally created to refer to people who were overly concerned with their own self-interest and ignored the needs of the community.
3. John 1:1–3.

2. *Gnostic Meaning*

Growth and *Construction*

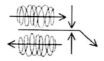   ('Jerusalem' and 'Babylon')

3. *Magical Meaning*

The law of the lightning bolt

(*a*) Lightning is produced by friction between two worlds. Whoever creates a *structure* not in harmony with heaven, creates a cloud in heaven—*seeds a thunderstorm.*)

Decadence is the effect of sustained and prolonged 'lightning' (Eliphas Lévi's principle of 'magical enchantment').

Mental, artistic, and physical *sterility* is not merely a *deficiency* but a *wound* caused by lightning, which is due in turn to a disharmonious encounter with reality.

(*b*) The great danger of occultism and practical magic is this: that one forces an encounter with a superior reality, which may however prove disharmonious (><), bringing on a *lightning bolt*, one effect of which is *sterility* and the other *insanity* (illusory productivity) (Nietzsche–Superman); in other words, an inferiority complex (sterility—distaste for life, pessimism, melancholy) or a superiority complex— *megalomania*, mania grandiosa (deluded messianism, illusory pretensions, 'Grand Master'—*madness*).

The Tower

The *two figures* tumbling down, one with a *crown—megalomania—* and the other, nearly horizontal—the sterility of *pessimism*.

4. Philosophical Meaning

Theory and experience (outer and inner); *truth* as an absolute *constructed system* (edifice) and truth as *unity* that *grows* through outer *and* inner experience, from above and from below (organism).

Univocal ideas and *symbols* (overdecked—open to what is above).

Closed circuits of systems and ideas lead inevitably to explosion: one *must* rest content with being but *half* and to possess only *half*—'man' and 'woman'—active construction, and passive reception of *revelation*; activity *and* receptivity.

The 'androgyny' of systems and ideas that are *closed* (as in XV) and sufficient unto themselves is *shattered* by experience. Symbols, on the contrary, are true 'androgynes': here one half is illuminated, and the other in shadow.

 *Moon (nocturnal light)*

This is the *collaboration* of the masculine and the feminine principles, their *marriage*, and not their unnatural union.

Just as a masculine woman or an effeminate man is a negative phenomenon, so also systems and ideas *deprived of any tendency* toward the 'other'—toward the higher or more comprehensive— are monstrosities. They are 'Towers of Babel', ambitions for and pretensions to *plenitude*, which however they are not.

Symbols are the androgyny of *sacred marriage*, one of the *seven* sacraments—wherein man remains man, and woman remains woman (each becoming such to a *greater degree* than before) while yet *completing* each other through their union in love and mutual

85

trust: here clear, active thinking and the reception of profound revelations *cooperate*, without thinking becoming vague and obscure or deep feeling turning into a clear and precise 'program' or 'system'.

5. *Esoteric Meaning*

(Those who would elevate themselves will be *humbled*; those who humble themselves will be raised up.)

Truth is Day *and* Night,
consciousness *and* superconsciousness,
effort *and* grace

One can neither build it [truth] nor possess it as a finished and completed structure: it must be created unceasingly by the *'fire from above'*—this is the *orientation* in all problems and tasks, but not a personal *possession* at own's own disposal.

Experience, Philosophy, Religion—they must unite in the quest for truth. An irreligious person is incapable of this, as also is someone who cannot think; for the one apprehends nothing of inner experience and the other nothing of outer experience.

XVII

The Star

Astra inclinant, non necssitant
[The stars incline, they do not compel]
Spes infirmum
[Hope of the sick]

A. LAYOUT OF THE CARD

Following the arcanum of decadence (XVI)—that of *re-establishment*. The stars, through the intermediary of the true (naked) feminine, render earthly life fruitful.

B. General Meaning

The unconscious (in the sense of C.G. Jung) unites the consciousness (the 'Day') of the human being with the starry world. In this way the aridity (fatigue, sterility, senility) of terrestrial life (day consciousness) is rendered fertile in the silence of the 'nocturnal' realms of consciousness *or* in sleep. The liquid that nourishes—keeps alive—the soul is *Hope*.

C. 1. Soul astrology—as the wisdom of Hope. *Astra inclinant, non necessitant*—this is the 'eighth planet' in the horoscope, which

87

determines the *choice* of the seven astral influences and is thus the concrete *hope* in every constellation. It is the 'transcendental Self'. It is 'Dharma' in the domain of 'Karma'.

2. *Heredity*—seen in the day of the wisdom of Hope: the 'eighth planet' in the hereditary constellation. *Hereditas inclinat, non necessitant* [Heredity inclines, it does not compel].

3. *Health (medicine)*—seen through the wisdom of Hope: the 'eighth planet' in the constellation, that is, the 'humors' (hormones) and glands. *Glandulae inclinant, non necessitant* [The glands incline, they do not compel].

4. The 'occult physiology' of *nephesh* and *ruach*:
The 'eighth lotus' (*chakra*). (Lotus [*Padma*]: Steiner, Vivekananda, A. Avalon, Alice A. Bailey, etc., see Arcanum VII). *Flores lotus inclinant, non necessitant* [The lotus flowers incline, they do not compel].

5. To be 'chosen' or 'condemned' (predestination) in Theology:

Salus infirmorum [salvation of the sick]. *Refugium peccatorum* [refuge of sinners], *Consolatrix afflictorum* [consoler of the afflicted]: the mystical *Mantle* of the Virgin ("judge *me* instead of them"— preposition) *Gratia gratis data: Malum et Bonum inclinant, non necessitant—nulla praedestinatio, sed spec omnibus* [Grace given gratuitously: Good and Evil incline, they do not compel—no predestination, but hope for all].

The XVIIth Arcanum refutes *determinism* in all domains— astrology, heredity, physiology, inner karmic constellation, and theology; it offers grounds for *Hope*. It is the VIIIth repeated: Justice includes grace, Hope (17 = 8 = 'eighth planet').

D. 1. Mystical Meaning

The starry Mantle of the Mother

2. *Gnostic Meaning*

Mediatrix mundi [World Intercessor]—

HEVAH, Sophia, Maria:
Virgin, Queen, Mother
SOPHIA

3. *Magical Meaning*

Magical medicine—the use by the Mage ('eighth planet') of the *healing* forces of the 7 planets; the use of the *great cosmic pharmacy* by the magician-doctor, the magician-pharmacist, and the magician-nurse.

Healing 'mantrams' and 'setrams'.

4. *Philosophical Meaning*

The philosophy of medicine: holism—the world as an organic whole, the human being as an organic whole; *vis mediatrix naturae* [the healing power of nature]. The philosophy of errors, vices, sins, and illnesses—and the methods of knowledge of the truth, of perfecting oneself morally, of the expiation of sins, and of the re-establishment of health.

5. *Esoteric Meaning*

Medicina universalis—the universal remedy (panacea): the *ensouled Word* (Logos *and* Sophia—*through* Sophia) moving the seven healing forces of the planets.
Healing through *union* with this Word:
(stages) truth, consolation, peace, joy—(accepting the truth, consolation through the truth, peace resulting from complete consolation, and joy resulting from the peace) with their physical analogues: the healing mystery of the Night (the super-consciousness).

89

The Night of Christmas: the Word is born solely *in* and *through* the Virgin; it is the same in the individual inner life.

The impoverishment of humanity caused by Protestantism: without the Mother the Word is not ensouled, and consequently humanity is deprived of the effect of the *Universal Remedy*. Christ becomes a Master who only *teaches*, not a Universal Healer. (The first miracle of St. John—the Wedding at Cana—indicates this law: there the miraculous deeds of the Son *are born* through the Mother.)

Note: the XXth Arcanum, which Eliphas Lévi treats as Universal Medicine, is more than medicine, since it is a matter not of healing but of *resurrection*—an absolutely *new beginning*.

XVIII

The Moon

Magic of the Past

Note: XVIII is a reflection of IX (but the Hermit has become the crayfish; his lantern is the Moon; his protection—the mantle—the dogs; and his support—the staff—is the towers): *the solitary life, the world of solitude*.

XVIII is also *determinism*, the antithesis of XVII, Hope, in its *triple* determinism:

spiritual—Moon (reflection) and towers (limits);
soul—the dog and the wolf (domestication and wildness—obedience, rebellion);
physical—crayfish (hard shell—separation from the world by the body).

Stagnation as the antithesis of the emanations of the stars of *XVII*.

A. LAYOUT OF THE CARD

Eclipse of the Moon—it is, then, the *Moon* itself, and not the reflection of the Sun's light.

The projection of the terrestrial into the heavens: the drops 'fall' up toward the Moon; the towers rise up (the same towers destroyed by the lightning bolt in card *XVI*!), the dogs—or dog and wolf—howl, the terrain is hilly and rounded, and from the pool rises its denizen—the crayfish. As for the Moon, the *human being* is projected onto it.

And the blue, red, and white rays encircling the eclipsed Moon?

They are the Moon's *own influence*, which persists even when it is eclipsed; that is, when it reflects as in a mirror the *Earth* instead of the Sun. Therein lies the essence of this Arcanum, and this is the reason why it is called 'The Moon'.

The card has, then, two aspects:

1. mirror of the Earth (of humanity and animality),
2. radiance (action) of the Moon *itself*, whence its:

B. General Meaning

The message of the Moon, when the terrestrial *present* eclipses its *future* (the reflection of the coming Sun), is the *past* that it revives. Memories, reminiscences of the past, are the radiance of the Moon in its own right.

N.B. Reminiscences are the *remedy* (as in card XVII) against terrestrial darkness, when this prevails.

[The present—the droplets 'falling' toward the Moon—depart the Earth for the Moon, but in return the *Past* radiates from the Moon; and the crayfish, whose mode of propulsion is inverse to that of Nature, is the reflection in the water of what is taking place above.]

Memory is the only light (colored) *at the hour of total darkness.*

It has three principal forms:

1. colored light (surrounding the Moon)
2. soul apathy (the dogs)
3. retrograde (backward) movement in the depths of the unconscious (the crayfish in the pond).

(1) *Plato* teaches that all knowledge is recollection, that is, *vertical* memory.

(2) *C. G. Jung* teaches that there is an historical memory in the collective unconscious—humanity's past (the primeval mysteries and primordial gnosis haunt the human soul [haunt—not only by the collective historical past, but also by the individual's past—by previous lives]); this is vertical and horizontal memory—*the cross of memory.*

(3) Biology teaches that instinctual life preserves the memory of the preceding stages of development—the ability to learn through the species—and the principle of heredity. This memory is *horizontal* only.

Knowledge, psychic state (healthy or unhealthy), and biological life are grounded in memory in the following ways.

$$|, +, —$$

The Crayfish = —
The Dog = +
The Moon's radiance = |

These three forms of memory are those of the terrestrial *night*—they do not include either revelation from above (of the past, present, or future—prophetic) or new *experiences* through the outer or inner senses. (The stars and the *Sun* represent the latter).

Since memory is always of the past and is concerned only with accomplished facts, it has also the aspect—this being its negative aspect—of *determinism*:

—spiritual determinism (Plato: spiritually one is only what one has done; one can know only what one has already known);
—psychic determinism (*Jung*: the determinism of psychic life by the 'archetypes');
—biological determinism (the evolutionary past). In this sense card XVIII is the antithesis of Hope, XVII.

But the two cards have in common that *Providence* serves *Fatalism* (or determinism) through the (white) light of remembrance. If one is not free in the sphere of lunar influences, one cannot *remember freedom*; the memory of the freedom—albeit paradisal—of the past reawakens.

Thus XVII is the action of *liberty* in service to Providence within the domain of fatalism (determinism), as the 'eighth planet'.

XVIII is the action of *Fatalism* (determinism through the past) in service of Providence as recollection.

XIX is the action of Liberty *and* Providence united—there is only liberated Providence or providential Liberty; the darknesses (shadows) of Fatalism are dissipated—*the Sun*.

XX is still more than providential Liberty or liberated Providence—it is the pinnacle of the magic of *grace*, or *Providence alone*, which works *after* it has united with human freedom.
It *surpasses* even liberty united with Providence: the *Resurrection*—or the *Judgment*.

C. *1. Mystical Meaning*

Religion (*Enoch* erected the first altar) as *remembrance*. *Ritual* as a means to combat forgetting.

2. Gnostic Meaning

Beginning and End are one.

3. Magical Meaning

The magic of the *past*: to reawaken memories and re-enliven the past (ritual, ceremony, mystery drama, identification).

4. Philosophical Meaning

The transcendental method

5. *Esoteric Meaning*

The loftiest memory—is Love.

I am the Alpha and the Omega, that is to say, "I make the past present (remembrance) and the future present (prophecy)."

Why do most Christians not remember the past (previous lives)? Because they *do not love* the past. One has to *love* the 'pagan' past.

XIX

The Sun

Providential Liberty or Liberated Providence

Note: XIX is the first Arcanum of the quaternity of synthesis: XIX (10 = 1); XX (20 = 2); XXI (21 = 3); and XXII (22 = 4).

It is the third unity; 1, 10, 100 (19).

It is the *manifestation and realization* of the intuition of the Magician and the answer to the question of the Sphinx: the true androgyne, perfect union, neither passive nor active, no longer superior or inferior—and perfect certitude in resplendent light.

A. LAYOUT OF THE CARD

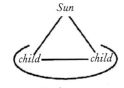

Enclosure—
"Construction without Obstruction"
(Paul Marteau)

or

96

The Sun

B. General Meaning

[*Pistis Sophia*: when the two become one...]
True androgyny—
Union in *the Sun above* (the human Heart in full bloom) and double polarization *below*.

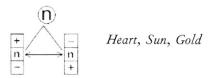

Heart, Sun, Gold

The problem of true *happiness*: sun-filled life.

Beatitude is not contemplation of God (eternal ecstasy), but seeing and acting in the world in divine light, warmth, and divine life. It is the cup filled with life—with happiness. Eternal *youth*.

The problem of *knowledge* of the truth: life in the light. One does not know all things, but one sees everything one encounters in the light of truth. Life lived in clarity, unburdened by the weight of prior experiences.

It is the antithesis of XVIII—of remembrance. It is no longer needed; one sees clearly in the *present*, in present *clarity*, that which is present—fresh and spontaneous creative knowledge. The stage of the naïveté of wisdom: the wisdom of the *child*. Absolute synthesis, but not as an ever-present system—which would be a prison—but as *light*, as vision. Things are seen in their unity; the unity is *given*.

C. 1. Mystic Meaning

The Son:
Sacred Heart of Jesus

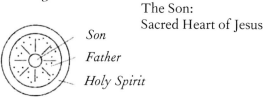

Son

Father

Holy Spirit

97

2. *Gnostic Meaning*

The Sun of Paradise (Garden),
of Heaven (Repose),
of the New Jerusalem (City).

3. *Magical Meaning*

The divine magic of the *Saints*—identification with God (Sun above), with one's fellow human beings (their vivification by the Sun), and with nature (its redemption).

The saints *give* life, and *take on* sickness—exchange.

Thus—never any stagnation: light *flows*, that being its law, the law of *solar magic*.

4. *Philosophical Meaning*

The essence of idealism: the subject draws from the source common to itself and its object.

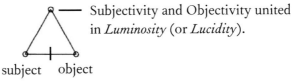 — Subjectivity and Objectivity united in *Luminosity* (or *Lucidity*).

subject   object

Metaphysics *is* possible—it is participation in the consciousness of the Logos "who is the light of the world," and by whom "all things were made," and "without whom was not anything made."

5. *Esoteric Meaning*

 "Where two *or* three are gathered in my name, there am I in their midst." [Matt. 18:20] I and Thou. The idea of the Church. *Extra Ecclesiam non est salus.*

98

The Sun

 umbra, penumbra, and light—
the Sun shines for everyone—physically and
spiritually.

The organism (*corpus mysticum*) of humanity—there is no healing
if it be not for all.

Extra ecclesiam non est salus—soli; sine solo non est salus—ecclesiae
[Outside the Church there is no salvation—for the individual;
without the individual, there is no salvation—for the Church].

The sacrament (mystery) of marriage—mystery of the Church—
mystery of androgyny—"where two or three are gathered in my
name, there am I in their midst."

XX

Judgment (Resurrection)

Magic of the Past
The Arcanum of Memory
—resurrection *and* judgment

Note: 20 is 2 and 11 = Gnosis, Force, Resurrection.

The 'Book' becomes 'Force' and Force becomes renewal of Life. Or knowledge becomes moral character, and moral character becomes new vitality (*neshamah, ruach, nefesh*).[1]

A. LAYOUT OF THE CARD

(The Marseille Tarot of 1761 [Nicolas Conver], of Fautrier 1753–1793, and of Court de Gébelin)

A man and a woman *contemplate* the resurrection of a *third* person from a tomb.

---

1. *Neshamah*: the moral consciousness, the highest of the three grades of the soul. *Ruach*: the intellectual faculty, the middle of the three grades of the soul. *Nefesh*: the vital principle, the lowest of the three grades of the soul (*The Zohar*, Vol. II, translated by Harry Sperling and Maurice Simon [London: Soncino Press, 1956], p. 403).

Judgment (Resurrection)

The structure of the awakening forces:

   1. the Angel with the Trumpet (tone),
   2. maternal and paternal love,
   3. the calling forth of the one raised from the dead—from an *open* tomb.

(The man and woman are *outside* the tomb; only their child—an adolescent—is raised from the dead.)

B. General Meaning

The triangle of the call back to life:

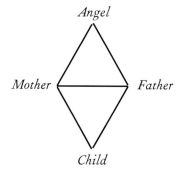

Angel

Mother *Father*

Child

The Father's love, the Mother's love, serving Memory's *power of recall* (Angel with Trumpet), effects the resurrection. The one raised from the dead, in face of such love, experiences at the same time the the situation of judgment (*Marteau*: he turns his back as a sign of the *secret*). *Judgment.*

Resurrection—victory over death (forgetting, sleep, and the state of absolute latency—the *amorphous* state, without form, or 'dead' in the strict sense)—through

   1. the awakening of memory (forgetting);
   2. the awakened memory awaking from sleep;
   3. *total awakening* signifying the re-establishment of *total life*—resurrection.

101

C. The Degrees of Resurrection

1. *Memory* (one forgets what one does not love; love is the force of memory; love grows, memory awakens—the past, previous lives, the history of humanity)—the *past*.

2. The *state of awakening* (one falls asleep, goes to sleep, when one forgets not only the past but also the *present*—when one finds nothing to do, nothing to see—*indifference to the present* is the sleep of the soul (also of the body).

The *state of wakefulness* (vigil) is that of *lively interest* in things of the present. Now, one takes no interest in things except through the power of Love. Whoever does not love, sleeps; whoever loves, awakens—the *present*.

3. The *state of the second life* (not biological) is that where the *future*, with its Work, its Mission, and its Goal are grown so present that the body itself, become one with the soul and the spirit—ensouled and spiritualized—no longer yields place to forgetfulness or indifference, to lethargic ignorance or the inactivity of death.

It does not draw vital force from the past, nor solely from the present, but also—and above all—from the *future*; *the future*.

The principle of *Memory* is the foundation of the entire process of resurrection; it is that which *recalls*, *awakens*, and *raises from the dead*: resurrection is the action of the 'Memory of the Future', awakening is the action of the 'Memory of the Present', and Remembrance in the action of the 'Memory of the Past'. But what is Memory?

It is love for the past, the present, and the future—*eternal Love*.

The Holy Trinity is not Power, Wisdom, and Love (as taught by St. Thomas, etc.)—it is nothing other than Love (St. John's "God is [total] love, and he who abides in love abides in God, and God abides in him" [1 John 4:16], namely:

conjugal love (the Wedding of the Lamb); *paternal* love (*Pater Noster qui es in coelis*... [Our Father who art in heaven...]); *maternal* love (*Sancta Maria, Mater Dei, ora pro nobis peccatoribus nunc et in hora mortis nostrae* [Holy Mary, Mother of God, pray for us sinners, now and in the hour of our death]; *filial* love (*Pater meus diligit me et ego diligo eum* [My Father loves me, and I love him]); and *fraternal* love (the Epistles are all addressed to the 'Brothers').

The Love of the Father-Mother is thus the creative power of Love (or God the Father); the Love of the Son is the filial love which is the wisdom of Love (or God the Son), and fraternal Love is the Love that establishes the Community of Beings (or the love of the Holy Spirit).

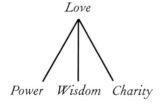

Love

Power   Wisdom   Charity

Here we have unity 'in substance' (which is Love) and the difference 'in the [three] persons' (which are the eternal modes of Love in the Past—Father, 'the Ancient of Days', the 'Ancient One'; of Love in the Present—the Son, "Before Abraham was, I am";[2] and of Love in the Future—the Holy Spirit, *Docebit omnem veritatem* [He will *teach* you all things][3]—of the Holy Trinity.

The Rosicrucian formula: *Ex Deo nascimur, in Christo morimur, per Spiritum Sanctum reviviscimus*—is the magical formula of the *Holy Trinity*—of God in eternity, *acting* according to the triple modality of Love: Past—Father; Present—Son; Future—Holy Spirit.

2. John 8:58
3. John 14:26

D. The Resurrection Body

Living body—nothing mechanical; body of *wakefulness*—nothing that *separates* ('skin'), or that renders indifferent; body of *memory*—nothing that lets one forget—*synthesis of the past.*

Body of Love, synthesis of Death and Life—being liberated as one dead; capable of acting as one living.

E. 1. Mystical Meaning

Perpetual resurrection—the mystery of renewal: the seven sacraments as seven aspects of resurrection.

2. Gnostic Meaning

The 'Book of Life'—World Memory, 'Akashic' Chronicle—which contains only what has value for eternity, what is worthy of resurrection.

3. Magical Meaning

The resurrecting magic of Memory: as a help for the dead, the living, the strayed, the sick—drawing from the spring of paternal, maternal, conjugal, filial, fraternal love: the veritable 'blazing star' of true magic.

 Such is the sign of this magic.

4. Philosophical Meaning

Historical 'renaissances' of ideas and cultural values:
Aristotelianism—thirteenth century
Platonism—fifteenth century, etc.

Judgment (Resurrection)

The problem of the history of philosophy: the cyclical continuity of 'renaissances'.

Platonism and Aristotelianism are eternal. 'Realism' and 'nominalism' (species–individualities) are eternal.

The Kabbalah and Hermeticism are also eternal—in their cyclical renaissances (thirteenth, sixteenth, seventeenth, eighteenth, nineteenth centuries).

5. Esoteric Meaning

The alchemical idea of the Rose-Cross:

Per Crucem ad Rosem [through the Cross to the Rose]; every sacrifice—becoming empty—is followed by a replenishment of the void with a new fullness.

Law of the strait way—concentration (renunciation), ☉ sacrifice—followed by the action of magic—homeopathy, the Way of the Cross. *Per mortem tuam mundum vivifiscasti* [through your death you have given life to the world].

Sacrifice is the foundation of High Magic—of the force of magic—which works together with the forces of resurrection.

105

XXI *or* ZERO *or* XXII
The Fool (The Jester)

Note: The Fool is one who has lost his memory, who has forgotten everything: the Fool is one who has 'memory of the future' and has forgotten the past and present; the Fool contemplates eternity and lives outside time.

The card is a reflection of III and XII: 'spiritual procreation' renders him 'hanged' and makes him appear a 'fool'—or it can be a reflection of IV and XIII: the 'dead' emperor—whose kingdom is not of this world.

The Fool is also the ר of ל 19 (Sun) and of ה (Judgment)—the carefreeness of a *sun-drenched newborn*.

A. LAYOUT AND GENERAL MEANING OF THE CARD

The dazzled?
The carefree?
The radical representative of that which is above; one who is set ablaze by the celestial fire?

In view of the level and context of the major Arcana of the Tarot, pure and simple 'folly' does not suffice, just as Cervantes' Don Quixote is not merely a case of folly. Don Quixote de la Manche wished to be a knight-errant at a time when there were no longer knights.

And the Fool (or 'The Jester' of Fautrier's Tarot) who wears the garb of a court jester, is he not a wanderer, a pilgrim to nowhere, an exile from everywhere, who cares not to appear as anything in particular, who want no name or glory or authority or power or wealth or home or parents or friends?

Is it not folly in the eyes of the world to despise all these things? You say: How would someone *look* who has understood the vanity of all personal claims to honor, position, authority, or power. Like a sage? Like a fool?

Jung made the important discovery that we all wear a psychological mask, a *persona*. But what 'persona' remains to those who strip themselves of this, who are nothing but *human beings*? What 'persona'—psychological garb—can be attributed to such ones?

That of the *Fool*.

It is the *ecce homo* [behold the man]. For in those days also they wrapped Him in a purple cloak, placed a staff in His hand, and crowned Him with thorns—for *His kingdom was not of this world.* Jacob Boehme: "You still say that you will be taken for a fool, which is true, for the Way that leads us to the love of God is folly to the world."

The Fool is the footloose Bohemian, the Exile, the Expatriate, the Cosmopolitan, the one who has abandoned the struggle for existence, who wants neither to conquer nor to defend anything, who cares not to persuade anyone of anything—*this is the free human being*.

And in the eyes of the world the only *garb* fit for a free human being is that of the Fool.

And "this is also true" because such a one is not a king or a knight or a soldier or a lawyer or a merchant or an artisan or a peasant or a bishop or a priest or a monk—what garb, then, is left for such a one but that of the Fool?

For *without garb* of some sort one cannot be on this earth. One has to wear something.

What is the cloak of the Hermit (IX), the cloak of Apollonius of Tyana, the cloak of the Pythagoreans? What do we find beneath this cloak? What does it conceal, what does it cover?

The Fool's garb.

The *cloak* of Apollonius of Tyana and of the Pythagoreans is the 'persona' (professional, as the *philosophers* of that time put it) which one puts on in order to hide the Fool from the world's view.

Why? So that people do not *imitate* it, for they are able to go and imitate *true freedom* without being free: and then they would become crazy through another *folly*—revolutionary rage and madness.

The State authorities have always suspected 'philosophers'—those with cloaks—of subversive influences.

Socrates was condemned to death, and all the philosophers were exiled from Rome by imperial decree under the emperor Justinian.

And the first Christians—as Justin Martyr attests—were seen (and they accepted this)—as 'philosophers', that is to say as cloaked Fools. What else could they do, seeing that the Apostle to the Gentiles, St. Paul, freely declared that it is a matter of folly in the Christian faith: "Jews demand signs [miracles] and Greeks seek wisdom, but we preach Christ crucified: a stumbling block to Jews and folly to Gentiles" (I Cor. 1:22–23).

The Fool (The Jester)

B. 1. Mystical Meaning

Love of God; ecstasy (St. Bonaventure)

2. Gnostic Meaning

Resurrection before the beginning of time, being raised from the dead (XX) before the universal resurrection: the Eternal *in* Time: resurrection *anticipated* in the soul in a world (and a body) that is fallen (the dog).

The *Threshold*—or the abyss separating the two domains: the *tension* of their antagonism being too great, the *threshold* is *guarded*.

3. Magical Meaning

The *Journey*—the magical Pilgrimage.

Magical 'postures': standing, sitting, kneeling, prostrating oneself, *walking*: it is the *vertical* that moves itself *horizontally* without *becoming horizontal*. 'Inscription' through movement—magical 'formulas' inscribed through a pilgrimage or 'journey'.

4. Philosophical Meaning

Illusion and reality.
Maya and the real.
The relative and the absolute.

5. Esoteric Meaning

The *Way* that is not a way (Lao Tzu).
The *Name* that is not a name.
The *Wisdom* that is not human wisdom.

There are no *methods*: there are only *preparations*; those who find the *way*, become *themselves* the way ('esoteric schools').

There are no ranks (names) or 'degrees' (3, 33, 99) to be *attained*—one cannot *attain* anything, or *arrive* anywhere: one can do nothing but *evolve*, be purified through fire, growth, and maturation (esoteric 'development and progress'—'masters', etc.).

There are no 'missions' to choose or to confer upon oneself: they are conferred, and may change from one hour to the next. The only enduring mission is *obedience* ('Leaders of humanity, missions', etc.).

The Fool is obedient to heaven, for everything is magic: one who cultivates a garden can accomplish a magical work of greater compass than one who evokes the seven planetary genii.

It can also be enough to *walk*, for Heaven to be actively present.

XXII (XXI)

The World

(The mystery of joy)

Note: The World and the Fool—XXI and XXII—are cards whose placements are interchangeable, just as the World is numbered XXI in the Tarot of Marseilles.

Thus the Fool is 4, 13: and as 1 (א) is found in every number (every number is an *aspect* or *fraction* of unity), so the kabbalistic name for the Fool is אדם—*Adam* or 'ecce homo'; whereas the World, taken as XXI, is the third manifestation of III, the Empress, and XII, the Hanged Man—the generative power from above to below ▽ (Hanged Man).

And if the Fool is Zero, he is the whole series of the Arcana, and the 21 Arcana are nothing but his *biography*: *each* Arcanum can be applied to him.

At the same time the World is *either* the *third* term of the quaternity Sun, Judgment, World, Fool, *or* the *fourth* term of the quaternity Son, Judgment, Fool, World. In the first case, it is *Joy* that results from the Sun and the Resurrection, while it is the Fool who experiences the joy of contemplation of the solar resurrection. In the second case, the World is the second *Hé* [of the Tetragrammaton]

111

that wholly encompasses the Sun, the Resurrection, and the Fool (vivifying power, resurrection, and the one raised from the dead)—which is to say that it is the *Life* that comprises Love (the Sun), Love's action (the Resurrection), and the Loved One (the Fool); or again, *Joy* as the essence, the quintessence (*quinta essentia*) of life, which manifests itself as fire, air, water, and earth.

A. And the LAYOUT OF THE CARD Confirms

What has just been explained, which is that the fifth essence—at the center of the four elements—is Joy: by dancing the naked woman directs with her magic wand the circle of blossoming life whose manifestation is the four elements which surround it.

The configuration is, then:

 = 6 : 4 elements,
the blossoming circle.
the Dancing Woman with the wand, or wands.

B. General Meaning

Joy is the essence of what lives; life is *Joy*.

The 4 elements are the ideal (Angel), enthusiasm (Eagle), élan (Lion), and persistence (Bull) of the Joy at the heart of all blooming, *growth*—or *life*.

Henri Bergson saw only the 'vital élan' as the motivating force of creative evolution—he saw only the Lion of our card.

Charles Darwin saw only the instinct for the *preservation* of the species—the Bull of our card.

H. P. Blavatsky presented in her *Secret Doctrine* a cosmic evolution moved by the universal desire for *liberty*—the Eagle of our card.

The World

The Judeo-Christian Tradition (Edgar Daqué[4] being a spokesman thereof in the field of biology) teaches that every creature aspires to reintegration with its universal archetype: which is the *human being*, who is the image and likeness of God, of which all beings are only partial and imperfect manifestations—this is the Angel of our card.

So we find in all things living the 'fire' of joy of the ideal, the 'air' of joy of enthusiasm for liberty, the 'water' of joy of the exuberant vital élan, and the joy, finally, of the 'earth' of the preservation and stability of existence. But at the heart of all that lives is Joy—and if one knows the essence of life, the essence of the World, one has Nietzsche's *Joyful Wisdom* (*Fröhliche Wissenschaft*).

Is this not Eve, HEVA, the unfallen 'Mother of everything living'? And is it not she with whom, in his wanderings, the Fool, Adam, ADM, has become enamoured?

"The Eternal Feminine draws us onward" (Goethe, *Faust*): it is the Fool who senses, or has a *presentiment* of, the Eternal Feminine—that is why he has nothing to do with the rest and is oblivious to the dog that bites him. The Fool is the Emperor of Death (Father of Death) (consciousness—pole of Death)—Adam; the World is the Empress of Life (Mother of everything living)— Eve (vitality—in contrast to consciousness).

What then is the general meaning not only of this card but also of all 22 Greater Arcana of the Tarot?

It is the Mystery of ADAM–EVE

—of the World Spirit, who if alone is Death and the Fool: for he lacks life, *Shakti*;

4. German paleontologist whom is cited in *Meditations on the Tarot*, 'The Wheel of Fortune', p235 in US edition, as advancing "the postulate of the pre-existence . . . of a prototype for all beings, which is the final as well as the effective cause of the whole process of evolution…"

—of the World Soul, who if alone is *Life* and the naked Dancing Woman: for she lacks the Way, the guidance of *Purusha*.

The Fool *walks*—the World *dances*. But the *Truth* that unites the *Way* and the *Life*, the wandering Fool and the dancing World, is the Great Arcanum of the 22 Arcana of the Tarot—the Word comprising these 22 letters.

And when the Wanderer and the Dancer join together in the Sun, like the two children of card XIX, not as the ones raised from the dead but as the Father and Mother who raise from the dead (from card XX), then this will be the *Truth* of their being rediscovered.

Then does the Dancing Woman become the Virgin Mother, and the Wanderer become the Virgin Father.

B. Mystical Meaning

Such is the general meaning of this card (and of the Major Arcana of the Tarot), which is at one and the same time its mystical, gnostic, magical, philosophical, and esoteric meaning.

C. Note on the Minor Arcana

Are the (4 x 14 =) 56 Minor Arcana the direct continuation of the Major Arcana (Arcanum 23, 24, etc.), or are they a new cycle, the 'second volume' of the Book of Thoth? And if the latter, do they represent the *involution* of the Major Arcana, or, rather, their *evolution*?

Both at the same time.

From the point of view of the *Game* and of practical *Divination* they are an *involution*—the trump-cards [the Major Arcana] are superior to them. This is the *exoteric* point of view.

From the *esoteric* point of view they are *superior* (evolution) to the Major Arcana.

The World

In what way?

They are a system of *meditation*, of spiritual exercises, in which the 'alphabet' of 22 'letters' is to be applied.

They require, moreover, a greater effort of consciousness than do the Major Arcana—the Kabbalah, Pythagoreanism must be explored at a deeper level—in order to draw from them teachings regarding the *practical way* of the ascension of consciousness through the 'four worlds' or 'initiatic degrees':

δόχα — [doxa]: *objective* consciousness (opposition of subject and object); or that of *opinions* or *ideas* (pentacles / coins).

διάνοια

[dianoia]: *penetrative*—or *critical*—consciousness, which puts to the test the hypotheses, opinions, and ideas of the preceding degree (swords).

ἐπιστήμη [episteme]: *intuitive* consciousness, which *receives* into itself the *substance* of the object—as a vessel receives liquid (cups).

Θεουργεία [theourgeia]: *creative* consciousness which *reveals* or creates from out of the complete union of the subject with the object of consciousness (*unio mystica*)—(wands).

1 and 2 lead to *vision*;

3 leads to *inspiration* (hearing);

4 leads to *intuition* (touch).

Now, the 4 x 14 Arcana provide a system of meditative exercises directed to the attainment of the higher degrees of consciousness.

The 22 Arcana are the 'sephirotic pathways'; the 4 x 14 Arcana are the *Sephiroth* themselves in the 4 worlds (*atʒiluth*, *briah*, *yetʒirah*, and *assiah*).

For our part, a study of the 'minor' Arcana would be possible only if the study of the 'major' Arcana were taken up by a wide enough circle of 'unknown friends' engaged in serious work on the Tarot.

The Cards
of the
Major Arcana

LE BATELEUR
THE MAGICIAN

LA PAPESSE
THE HIGH PRIESTESS

L'IMPÉRATRICE
THE EMPRESS

L'EMPEREUR
THE EMPEROR

LE PAPE
THE POPE

L'AMOUREUX
THE LOVER

LE CHARIOT
THE CHARIOT

LA JUSTICE
JUSTICE

L'HERMITE
THE HERMIT

LA ROUE DE FORTUNE
THE WHEEL OF FORTUNE

LA FORCE
FORCE

LE PENDU
THE HANGED MAN

XIIII

TEMPÉRANCE
TEMPERANCE

XV

LE DIABLE
THE DEVIL

XVI

LA MAISON DIEU
THE TOWER OF DESTRUCTION

XVII

L'ÉTOILE
THE STAR

XVIII

LA LUNE
THE MOON

XVIIII

LE SOLEIL
THE SUN

XX

LE JUGEMENT
JUDGEMENT

XXI

LE MONDE
THE WORLD

LE MAT
THE FOOL

119

Printed by BoD™in Norderstedt, Germany